THE PILGRIM'S GUIDE TO SANTIAGO

The Roadmap to a Stress-Free and Unforgettable Camino

2025 EDITION

PLAN WITH CONFIDENCE AND CHOOSE THE ROUTE THAT'S RIGHT FOR YOU

© 2025 WanderLight Publishing All rights reserved. This guidebook is for informational use only. Trademarks and brand names are owned by their respective proprietors. Provided "as is," with no guarantees. Reproduction or distribution without permission is prohibited. The publisher is not liable for any damages from using or misusing the information herein.

TABLE OF CONTENTS

INTRODUCTION 9

Why The Ccamino? 10
Using This Guide For a Stress-free camino 10

PART I: YOUR CAMINO ESSENTIALS
CHAPTER 1: WHAT IS THE CAMINO DE SANTIAGO? 12

The Pilgrim's Journey: History and routes 13
Why Walk? Motivations for the Camino 14

CHAPTER 2:
PILGRIM CERTIFICATIONS MADE SIMPLE 15

Compostela and other pilgrimage certificates 16
The pilgrim credential 16
The new compostela rule 17

CHAPTER 3:
PLAN LIKE A PRO 18

Best Seasons for Every Route 19
Budgeting your camino 20
Budget breakdown example 21
Solo vs. group travel considerations 22

CHAPTER 4:
GEAR UP FOR SUCCESS 23

Lightweight, Smart, and Practical Packing 24
Seasonal packing essentials 25
Backpack, footwear, and gear 26

CHAPTER 5:
TRAINING FOR THE TRAIL 27

Preparing Your Body and Mind 28
Realistic plans to build stamina 29

PART II: CAMINO ROUTES 31

CHAPTER 6: CAMINO FRANCÉS 34

Most Popular Route: Historical Significance 35
Terrain, stops, and secrets 36
Landmarks and Insider Tips 38
Alternative routes to Santiago 40
Camino Aragonés 40
Camino del Ebro 41
Ruta de la Lana 43
Camino de Invierno 45

CHAPTER 7:
CAMINO PORTUGUÉS 47

Central vs. Coastal Routes Comparison 48
Cultural Treasures and Scenic Highlights 49
Practical Tips for a Smooth Journey 51
Avoiding Common Pitfalls 52
Camino Espiritual 53

CHAPTER 8:
CAMINO PRIMITIVO 55

Challenges and Rewards on the Oldest Route 56
Wild Terrain and Remote Beauty 57
What to Expect Along the Way 58
Essential Preparation Tips 59

CHAPTER 9:
CAMINO DEL NORTE 60

Coastal Beauty and Rugged Trails 61
Scenic Detours and Hidden Beaches 62

CHAPTER 10:
CAMINO INGLÉS 65

The Perfect Short Option for Beginners 66
Solo Walking: Highlights and Safety Tips 67
Practical Advice for Solo Traveler 68

CHAPTER 11:
VIA DE LA PLATA 70

Long Distances and Historic Paths 71
Daily Stages and Unique Challenges 72
Camino Sanabrés: A Direct Route to Santiago 74

CHAPTER 12:
BEYOND SANTIAGO 75

Walking to the End of the World 76
Coastal Reflections and Stunning Views 78
Practical Tips for This Optional Route 79

PART III: WALKING THE CAMINO
CHAPTER 13: NAVIGATING THE CAMINO CONFIDENTLY 80

Following Waymarks: Arrows, Shells, Signs 81
Using Apps for Stress-Free Walking 82
Avoiding Common Navigation Mistakes 83

CHAPTER 14: SAFE, COMFORTABLE, AND PREPARED 84

Safety Tips for Vulnerable Pilgrims 85
Emergency Actions on the Camino 86

Chapter 15: Accommodations and Dining 88

Choosing the Right Accommodation 89
Budget-Friendly Dining Strategies 90

Part IV: Enriching Your Experience
Chapter 16: The Culture of the Camino 92

Pilgrim Rituals & Traditions 93
Symbolism of Shell, Staff, & Scallop Markers 93
Modern-Day Pilgrim Community 94
Respecting Local Culture & Etiquette 95

CHAPTER 17: REFLECTING ON YOUR JOURNEY 97

Capturing Your Camino Memories 98
Camino Lessons for Daily Transformation 98
Staying Connected & Future Pilgrimages 99

BONUS
CAMINO SECRETS
Top Stays & Dining for Every Pilgrim

After a long day walking, finding a good place to rest and eat shouldn't be another challenge.

Why waste energy searching for a bed or wondering where to eat when you could have everything planned in advance?

That's why we created this essential guide with handpicked **accommodations** and **local dining spots, all at your fingertips.**

Inside you'll find trusted albergues and hotels, must-try pilgrim menus, and smart arrival strategies.

Scan the QR code below and walk the Camino with confidence!

INTRODUCTION

WHY THE CAMINO?

Walking the Camino de Santiago offers more than just a physical experience; it profoundly explores self, spirituality, and the rich history and culture surrounding this ancient pilgrimage route. The Camino, with its numerous paths leading to Santiago de Compostela, has long attracted those seeking adventure, a deeper connection to the past, and a chance for introspection. The significance of the Camino de Santiago goes beyond the act of walking; it represents a spiritual quest, cultural immersion, and personal challenge that draws individuals from around the world.

Spiritual Significance: For many, the Camino represents a spiritual path, fostering self-discovery and personal growth. This pilgrimage provides a unique opportunity to step away from the daily grind and engage in introspection and meditation. Rooted in Christian tradition, the route leads to the tomb of St. James the Apostle, yet it warmly invites people of all faiths and beliefs. Walking, embracing the simplicity of a pilgrim's life, and sharing experiences with fellow travelers cultivate a deep spiritual awakening and a sense of connection to something greater.

Cultural Significance: The Camino de Santiago acts as a living museum, offering a glimpse into the history, art, and traditions of the regions it passes through. Each route shares its narrative, from the architectural wonders and historic cities of the Camino Francés to the Celtic influences and rugged landscapes of the Camino Primitivo. Pilgrims gain firsthand experience of Spain's rich cultural heritage, including its languages, cuisines, and festivals, creating a vibrant tapestry of human expression.

Personal Significance: On a personal level, the Camino presents challenges that test individuals physically, emotionally, and mentally. This experience pushes one's limits and promotes self-improvement. Many choose the Camino during transitional life phases, seeking clarity, healing, or a sense of accomplishment. The path allows for solitude and community, enabling pilgrims to reflect inwardly while forming deep connections with fellow travelers from diverse backgrounds, leading to lifelong friendships and cherished memories.

Transformative Experience: The Camino de Santiago transforms lives. The lessons learned, challenges faced, and the simplicity of the pilgrim lifestyle leave a lasting impact, often resulting in significant personal growth and a new outlook on life. This experience fosters resilience, gratitude, and a deeper appreciation for life's simple joys.

The Camino de Santiago transcends mere trekking; it represents a journey of the soul, a cultural exploration, and a personal quest that offers each pilgrim a unique and transformative experience. Motivated by spiritual, cultural, or personal reasons, those who walk the Camino discover a path filled with challenges, beauty, and moments of profound insight. This rich array of experiences makes the Camino de Santiago a pilgrimage unlike any other, inviting travelers to engage in this life-changing experience.

USING THIS GUIDE FOR A STRESS-FREE CAMINO

This guide is your companion for navigating the Camino de Santiago easily and confidently. To ensure a stress-free experience, follow these steps:

1. Start with Your Why: Reflect on your motivation for this pilgrimage. Knowing your personal goals will help tailor the trip to your needs and keep you focused on the rewarding aspects of your experience.

2. Choose Your Route: Familiarize yourself with the Camino routes described in Part II. Consider factors like distance, scenery, and historical significance to select the path that resonates most with you, enhancing your overall experience.

3. Plan Your Timing: Consult Chapter 3 to determine the best season for your pilgrimage. Balancing weather preferences with crowd levels can significantly impact your experience, making it all the more enjoyable.

4. Budget Wisely: Create a realistic budget by using the thorough breakdowns in Chapter 3 to account for lodging, meals, and unforeseen costs. Being financially ready will let you enjoy the experience to the fullest without worrying about anything.

5. Pack Smart: Chapter 4 offers indispensable advice on packing essentials, ensuring you carry only what you need for comfort and safety without overburdening yourself. Thoughtful packing will empower you to focus on the path ahead.

6. Prepare Physically and Mentally: Chapter 5 provides training plans and mental preparation tips. Starting your pilgrimage in good physical shape and with a positive mindset is crucial for facing the challenges and joys that await.

7. Navigate with Confidence: Chapter 13 outlines how to follow the Camino's waymarks and use modern tools for stress-free navigation. Familiarize yourself with these resources before you depart to ensure you can navigate confidently.

8. Stay Safe and Comfortable: Safety tips and accommodation advice in Chapters 14 and 15 are essential for a comfortable experience, especially for solo travelers and those with specific needs. Being prepared can make all the difference.

9. Engage with the Culture: To enhance your Camino experience, read Chapter 16 for rich cultural insights and pilgrim traditions. Engaging with the local way of life will improve your stay and help you make lifelong memories.

10. Reflect and Document: Chapter 17 encourages you to think about your experience and offers tips for capturing memories, ensuring your Camino experience inspires you long after you return home. You can gain a deeper insight into your journey by taking the time to reflect.

Following these steps and utilizing the specific chapters as a roadmap will equip you with a clear plan and peace of mind for your Camino experience. This guide is designed for you to revisit at each stage of your preparation and journey, ensuring a seamless and transformative pilgrimage.

PART I: YOUR CAMINO ESSENTIALS

Chapter 1: What Is the Camino de Santiago?

THE PILGRIM'S JOURNEY: HISTORY AND ROUTES

The Way of St. James, also known as the Camino de Santiago, began when the grave of St. James the Apostle was allegedly found in northwest Spain in the early ninth century. Due to this important discovery, the little town of Santiago de Compostela became a major destination for Christian pilgrims, on par with Rome and Jerusalem. A system of roads grew throughout Europe over the ages, all of which led to this hallowed location. The pilgrimage promoted cultural interchange and understanding among the various peoples of medieval Europe and acted as a spiritual quest.

Several routes that make up the Camino have become well-known because they provide distinct insights into the histories, cultures, and landscapes of the areas they pass through. The most well-known is the Camino Francés, which connects Santiago de Compostela, Spain, with Saint-Jean-Pied-de-Port, France, over a distance of roughly 780 kilometers (485 miles). For many pilgrims, this route is the foundation of their Camino experience because of its well-established infrastructure and abundance of historical buildings. Its wide range of services and the strong sense of community it creates among people worldwide are the main reasons for its popularity, which makes it a friendly option for many.

The Camino Portugués, which has two primary routes—the Central Route and the Coastal Route—is another important route. The Central Route, which begins in Lisbon and travels around 610 kilometers (379 miles) through typical Portuguese cities and countryside, offers a glimpse into the country's vibrant culture and rich religious legacy. For those seeking the peace of coastal scenery and the revitalizing marine environment, the Coastal Route provides a picturesque trip along the Atlantic coast.

For the adventurous and those seeking isolation, the Camino del Norte and the Camino Primitivo offer more difficult terrain and less populated routes. The Camino del Norte, which stretches from Irún to Santiago along Spain's northern coast, highlights the untamed splendor of Galicia, Asturia, Cantabria, and the Basque Country. The original path to Santiago, the Camino Primitivo, offers a challenging but rewarding journey over the Asturian mountains, beckoning those prepared to take on its challenges.

The Camino Inglés is a shorter yet historically significant option for anyone with little time or who wants something less demanding. This less than 120-kilometer (about 75-mile) route, which starts in the English-speaking ports of Ferrol or A Coruña, is rich in the medieval custom of English and Irish pilgrims traveling to Spain to begin their pilgrimage.

Another significant route is the Via de la Plata, which follows historic Roman highways north from Seville in southern Spain to Santiago. This route, which is the longest of the Camino routes, encourages people to discover their inner potential and the history by providing a singular experience through the varied landscapes and cultural heritage of western Spain.

Each of these routes, with its distinct characteristics, challenges, and rewards, contributes to the rich tapestry of the Camino de Santiago. The tradition of walking the Camino, deeply embedded in European history, continues to evolve, attracting modern-day pilgrims from all walks of life. These travelers pursue the Camino for many reasons, from spiritual and religious motivations to personal growth and cultural exploration. The Camino de Santiago, with its blend of historical significance, cultural richness, and personal challenge, provides a transformative experience that resonates with the adventurous spirit of today's pilgrims. As they traverse these ancient paths, modern pilgrims connect with the past and a global community of like-minded individuals, each on their unique path toward self-discovery and fulfillment.

WHY WALK? MOTIVATIONS FOR THE CAMINO

Deciding to walk the Camino de Santiago combines one's personal, cultural, and spiritual aspects into a singular experience. Every pilgrim has a particular set of goals and seeks a different kind of fulfillment, which greatly influences their reasons for walking this ancient way. Understanding these drivers makes it easier for future pilgrims to understand why they are making this journey, which results in a more concentrated and significant experience.

The Camino offers a retreat from the noise and haste of modern life, inviting pilgrims into a space of reflection and connection. For many, it serves as a physical manifestation of a spiritual journey, a quest for deeper insights, or a way to honor a central tradition to Christian pilgrimage for centuries. Walking day after day creates a rhythm that can lead to profound moments of meditation and personal revelation. Pilgrims often report a sense of closeness to the divine, a reawakening of their faith, or newfound spiritual clarity when they reach Santiago de Compostela.

With its historical landscapes and architectural wonders from several eras, the Camino serves as a living museum of culture. People who walk the Camino can travel back in time and see the various historical eras that have influenced the areas it passes through. In a centuries-old ritual, pilgrims participate in local languages, customs, and culinary delights. This chance for cultural interchange and knowledge is unmatched, as it immerses oneself in the rich cultural tapestry of Spain and, depending on the itinerary, France and Portugal. Through mental expansion, the experience cultivates a greater understanding of the intricacies and beauties of diverse cultures.

On a personal level, motivations for walking the Camino vary as widely as the individuals themselves. Some view it as a challenge to meet, testing their physical and mental endurance.

Others see it as a chance to disconnect from the digital world and reconnect with nature or to process significant life events, such as the loss of a loved one, a career change, or a milestone birthday. The Camino offers a backdrop for personal narratives to unfold, providing space and time for introspection and self-discovery. This experience encourages pilgrims to confront their limitations, fears, and hopes, often leading to significant personal growth and transformation.

The objectives established before embarking on the Camino greatly influence the experience. A spiritually oriented pilgrim can choose less-traveled paths or slower seasons to find solitude. People with cultural interests may schedule their trip to take place during regional celebrations or make sure to see important historical locations. People who are driven by personal motives, on the other hand, might choose their starting locations and daily distances by striking a balance between challenge and self-care, giving them time and energy to contemplate.

By acknowledging and respecting these reasons, pilgrims can customize their Camino journey to achieve their goals, whether personal development, cultural immersion, or spiritual rejuvenation. The journey turns into a personal narrative interwoven with the greater Camino de Santiago story rather than being a physical track traveled by innumerable feet before theirs. They may make their Camino a transforming experience by starting with a clear grasp of their motivations, guaranteeing that every step they take will bring them closer to the desired transformation.

CHAPTER 2: PILGRIM CERTIFICATIONS MADE SIMPLE

COMPOSTELA AND OTHER PILGRIMAGE CERTIFICATES

The Compostela is a certificate of accomplishment given to pilgrims who have cycled at least the last 200 kilometers (about 124 miles) or walked at least the last 100 kilometers (about 62 miles) to Santiago de Compostela. Their personal, religious, or spiritual dedication is demonstrated by this certificate. As evidence that the pilgrim has visited St. James' tomb for significant religious or spiritual reasons, this beloved custom dates back to the Middle Ages. It was published by the Pilgrim's Office in Santiago de Compostela and is written in Latin. Pilgrims must obtain stamps in their Pilgrim's Credential, a document resembling a passport, to show their progress and stays at several locations throughout their journey to be eligible for the Compostela.

The Compostela holds significance beyond being a mere certificate; it symbolizes personal growth, endurance, and the fulfillment of a spiritual or personal quest. For many, receiving the Compostela evokes deep emotions, marking a significant milestone in their lives. It connects them to the millions of pilgrims who have traversed the same paths over centuries, weaving them into a continuous thread of human history and spirituality.

Other certificates can commemorate different aspects of the Camino experience. The Certificado de Distancia provides the exact distance a pilgrim has traveled on their journey to Santiago, offering a personalized record of their pilgrimage. This certificate, also issued by the Pilgrim's Office, includes the pilgrim's name, the start date of the pilgrimage, the starting point, and the total distance covered.

It is possible to earn extra certifications for pilgrims who continue their journey past Santiago de Compostela to Finisterre and Muxía. A sense of completion beyond the conventional endpoint is provided by the Finisterrana, which is given to individuals who reach Finisterre, traditionally thought of as the end of the known world. The Muxiana is also accessible to pilgrims who visit Muxía, a location of great historical and spiritual significance, especially concerning the Virgin Mary. These certificates recognize the pilgrims' commitment and the spiritual growth of their journey, just like the Compostela does.

To receive these credentials, one must fulfill certain requirements, such as gathering stamps from the places visited outside of Santiago in the Pilgrim's Credential. Beginning at the beginning of the Camino, the custom of stamp collecting extends to these additional locations, tying the entire journey together in a written format. The pilgrim's experience is enhanced by this procedure, which offers a tangible record of the journey and promotes interaction with nearby towns and locations.

The Compostela and other certificates play a crucial role in the Camino de Santiago experience, connecting the physical and spiritual aspects of the pilgrimage. They stand as a testament to the pilgrim's perseverance, faith, and personal transformation, encapsulating the essence of the pilgrimage in a document that can be cherished for years to come. For many, these certificates represent the symbols of profound experience that leave an indelible mark on their lives, connecting them to a tradition that spans centuries and a global community of pilgrims.

THE PILGRIM CREDENTIAL

The Pilgrim Credential, often referred to as the "Credencial del Peregrino," is a fundamental document for anyone participating in the Camino de Santiago. This passport-like booklet serves as a record of your journey and provides access to pilgrim-specific accommodations, ultimately qualifying you for the Compostela or other certificates of completion. For a smooth pilgrimage experience, it is essential to understand how to acquire, use, and properly complete this certification.

To obtain your Pilgrim Credential, start by contacting a local Confraternity of Saint James or a pilgrim's association in your country. These organizations support Camino pilgrims and can provide you with the credential for a small fee. If you begin your journey in Spain or another European country, many starting points of the Camino, such as Saint-Jean-Pied-de-Port in France or Roncesvalles and Sarria in Spain, have pilgrim's offices or local churches where you can acquire the credential upon arrival. Getting your credential before leaving for Spain is advisable, as it helps you start your pilgrimage smoothly.

Although using the credential is simple, it takes effort. Get stamps (sellos) in your credential from different places as you travel the Camino to show how far you've come. Numerous places, such as town halls (ayuntamientos), churches, hostels (albergues), and even a few cafes and restaurants along the way, sell these stamps. Generally speaking, you should acquire at least one stamp every day, but once you are within the final 100 kilometers (or the final 200 kilometers if you are cycling) of Santiago de Compostela, you must collect at least two stamps daily. This increase shows that you have completed the last and most important part of your trek; this encourages you to cross the finish line.

It is crucial to correctly complete the Pilgrim Credential. When you receive your credential, you will see sections for your details, such as your name, the date of your trip, and the starting location. Completing this section should be clear and readable. Make sure the date next to each stamp is correct and that the stamps are positioned in the appropriate locations as you collect them. These dates and stamps serve as a personal memento that records your singular experience and provides a chronological record of your journey, which is necessary to acquire the Compostela.

The Pilgrim's Office will check your completed Pilgrim Credential when you arrive in Santiago de Compostela. To confirm that you have fulfilled the requirements for obtaining the Compostela or other certifications, the dates and stamps will be carefully examined. To guarantee that your credential stays intact and readable so you can proudly display your well-earned accomplishments, it is crucial that you keep it dry and safe during your journey.

A key component of your Camino de Santiago journey is the Pilgrim Credential. To make sure your pilgrimage is acknowledged and rewarded when you arrive in Santiago de Compostela, get it from a reliable source before you set out, carefully gather stamps along the way, and accurately fill out your personal information. This document is a physical record of your spiritual, cultural, and individual experiences along this historic route and acts as your pass to the pilgrim-specific services along the Camino.

THE NEW COMPOSTELA RULE

In recent developments, the Pilgrim's Office has introduced a significant update to the rules for obtaining the Compostela, a change that accommodates a broader spectrum of pilgrims and acknowledges the diverse circumstances and capabilities of modern travelers. This new rule permits pilgrims to complete the requisite 100 kilometers (approximately 62 miles) to Santiago de Compostela in non-consecutive stages. This adjustment thoughtfully responds to the needs of those who may find it challenging to walk the traditional continuous path due to time constraints, physical limitations, or personal preferences.

This regulation provides flexibility, enabling pilgrims to travel the Camino in sections that suit their physical capabilities and schedules without compromising the pilgrimage's spiritual or personal significance. By being aware of this revised regulation, you may confidently navigate the experience and design a course that suits your unique situation.

Making a plan becomes crucial. Those pilgrims who choose non-consecutive walks should keep detailed records of every step they take, making sure they get the required stamps in their Pilgrim Credential for each one they finish. When presenting the Credential at the Pilgrim's Office in Santiago de Compostela, this paperwork acts as authentic proof of the pilgrimage.

Strategic route planning opportunities are made possible by this regulation. It is now possible for pilgrims to think about segmenting their journey into smaller, more manageable parts, possibly concentrating on various routes over many years or seasons. This method makes the Camino easier to reach and enables greater in-depth interaction with the wide range of villages, cultures, and scenery along the many routes. The Camino Francés, for example, has a rich history and a thriving pilgrim population. Later, one might tackle the Camino Primitivo's untamed splendor or the Camino del Norte's serene coastline setting.

Returning to the precise location where one left off is a logistical consideration as well. Careful planning is necessary for this, particularly for pilgrims traveling from abroad. Planning for transportation back to these locations for the subsequent leg of the trip is advised, as is keeping thorough notes of each segment's finishing sites, including GPS coordinates if possible.

A more introspective and customized pilgrimage experience is encouraged by the implementation of this guideline. Before proceeding to the next phase, pilgrims might pause and incorporate the knowledge and understandings they have gained from each section into their lives. By taking a piecemeal approach, the Camino can become a continuous process of spiritual and personal development rather than a one-time occurrence.

The Camino de Santiago is now much more accessible and inclusive according to the new Compostela regulation, which encourages a greater range of pilgrims to participate in this life-changing event. By permitting non-consecutive 100-kilometer treks, the Compostela can be reached flexibly, acknowledging the changing character of pilgrimage in the modern world. To ensure their experience stays personal and significant, pilgrims should embrace this opportunity with careful planning, strategic route selection, and a reflective mindset.

CHAPTER 3: PLAN LIKE A PRO

BEST SEASONS FOR EVERY ROUTE

Selecting the ideal time for your Camino de Santiago pilgrimage is crucial for a fulfilling experience. Each route offers unique landscapes, weather patterns, and cultural events, making some months more suitable than others. This guide breaks down the best seasons for each major Camino route, considering factors like weather, crowd sizes, and local festivals. This information aims to help you plan with confidence, allowing for full immersion in the spiritual, cultural, and personal growth opportunities the Camino provides.

Camino Francés: The most popular route, known for its well-established infrastructure and vibrant pilgrim community, sees the highest foot traffic from late spring to early fall (May to September). To avoid the peak summer crowds and the intense heat of July and August, consider walking in May, June, or September. These months offer pleasant weather, with fewer pilgrims and a chance to experience local festivals like the Fiesta de San Fermin in Pamplona in July.

Camino Portugués: The Central and Coastal paths of the Camino Portugués are best walked from March to June or from September to November. These periods avoid the scorching summer temperatures and the dense crowds of July and August. With pleasant temperatures that improve your strolling experience, the shoulder seasons offer the chance to see the harvest season in the fall and the blooming landscapes in spring.

Camino del Norte: The Camino del Norte, renowned for its breathtaking coastline vistas and difficult terrain, is best experienced from June to September. The driest weather occurs around this time, which is ideal for negotiating the rough roads. The path can be rather damp at certain times of the year, making certain parts challenging to travel. Additionally, local festivities along the coast are held in the summer, giving your journey a vibrant cultural component.

Camino Primitivo: The oldest route, characterized by its remote beauty and challenging mountain paths, is most accessible from June to September. Outside of these months, the weather can be unpredictable, with a higher chance of rain and even snow at higher elevations. Walking during the summer allows you to enjoy breathtaking landscapes with the safety of better weather conditions.

Camino Inglés: A shorter route ideal for beginners or those with limited time, the Camino Inglés can be comfortably walked from April to October. The milder climate of Northern Spain during these months offers a pleasant experience, avoiding the heavier rains typical of the region outside this window. This period also coincides with several local festivals, providing a rich cultural experience.

Via de la Plata: The longest route, stretching from Seville in the south of Spain to Santiago, is best walked during spring (March to May) or fall (September to November). These seasons avoid the extreme heat of the Andalusian summer, making the journey more comfortable. The spring bloom and autumn colors provide a stunning backdrop to the ancient Roman roads that define this path.

Finisterre and Muxía: For those extending their pilgrimage to the coast, the best time to visit Finisterre and Muxía is from May to September. This period offers the best chance for clear skies and mild weather, ideal for experiencing the dramatic coastal landscapes and sunsets. However, even during these months, be prepared for variable conditions, as coastal weather can be unpredictable.

General Considerations: Consider the local temperature, your weather preferences, and any religious or cultural festivals you choose to attend while organizing your Camino. The Camino is a symbol of spiritual and personal exploration in addition to a physical journey. Your choice of season can impact on everything from the people you meet to the scenery you see. Choosing the ideal time of year for your trip will depend on how you balance your needs for solitude or community, difficulty or ease.

Careful consideration of these factors allows you to tailor your Camino experience to match your personal goals and preferences, ensuring a memorable and transformative experience.

BUDGETING YOUR CAMINO

Planning your finances for the Camino de Santiago is crucial to ensure a fulfilling yet economical experience. This section highlights the key components of your budget: accommodation, food, and gear, providing a detailed breakdown of costs along with practical saving tips and strategies to maximize your budget.

ACCOMMODATION	FOOD	GEAR
The Camino offers a variety of sleeping options, from the communal atmosphere of albergues (pilgrim hostels) to the comfort of hotels and guesthouses. Your accommodation budget will depend largely on your preference for privacy and comfort.	Dining along the Camino serves as both a cultural exploration and a budgeting challenge. Many restaurants along the route offer pilgrim menus, featuring a three-course meal priced between $10 and $15. Opting for self-catering by purchasing food from local markets can lower your daily food expenses to less than $10.	Investing in quality gear is essential for a comfortable pilgrimage, but it doesn't have to be expensive. Focus your spending on footwear and a backpack, as these items will significantly impact your experience.
Albergues represent the most economical choice, with prices ranging from $10 to $20 per night for a bed in a shared dormitory. Many operate on a first-come, first-served basis, adding an element of spontaneity to your stay.	**Breakfast** usually consists of coffee, juice, and toast or pastries, costing around $3 to $5. A good breakfast can set a positive tone for your day!	**Footwear**: Durable, supportive walking shoes or boots are vital. Expect to spend $100 to $200 for a pair that will endure the journey and keep your feet comfortable.
Private rooms in guesthouses or small hotels typically cost between $40 and $100 per night, varying by location and season.	**Lunch and Dinner:** Pilgrim menus provide excellent value, but if you prefer cooking, groceries for a day can be as low as $10.	**Backpack:** A lightweight, well-fitted backpack is necessary. Suitable options range from $50 to $150.
		Additional Gear: Including clothing, rain gear, and a sleeping bag, can total $200 to $300.

Saving Tips and Budgeting Strategies

1. Book in Advance: For accommodations that accept reservations, booking ahead can secure better rates, especially outside of peak pilgrimage seasons.

2. Choose Albergues: Opt for pilgrim hostels for most of your stay to significantly reduce costs while connecting with fellow travelers.

3. Self-Cater: Purchase food from local markets and prepare your meals. Many albergues provide kitchen facilities, making meal prep a fun activity.

4. Travel Off-Peak: Walking during the shoulder seasons (spring and fall) can lower costs for both accommodation and flights to Europe.

5. Carry a Water Bottle: Refill at the numerous fountains along the route instead of buying bottled water, making hydration easy and budget-friendly.

6. Group Travel: Consider walking with friends or family to share the costs of private rooms and meals, creating lasting memories together.

BUDGET BREAKDOWN EXAMPLE

For a 30-day journey on the Camino Francés, a frugal pilgrim can expect to spend approximately:

- Accommodation: $300 to $600 (staying in albergues)
- Food: $300 to $450 (mix of self-catering and pilgrim menus)
- Gear: $350 to $650 (one-time purchase, can be used on future treks)
- Miscellaneous: $100 to $200 (laundry, toiletries, pharmacy items, and occasional treats)

This brings the total estimated cost from $1,050 to $1,900 for the pilgrimage, excluding airfare to and from the Camino. Remember that these figures are estimates; personal preferences and unexpected expenses can alter your budget.

Pilgrims can navigate the financial aspects of their experience with confidence, focusing on the spiritual, cultural and personal enrichment that the Camino de Santiago provides.

Traditional vs. Personalized Camino Routes

Choosing the Camino de Santiago presents pilgrims with a pivotal decision: follow the traditional routes that have been walked for centuries or customize the experience to suit personal preferences and comfort levels. This choice significantly affects the experience of the pilgrimage, influencing the landscapes you experience and the fellow travelers you meet along the way.

TRADITIONAL ROUTES

PROS:

- Well-Trodden Paths: The traditional routes, especially the Camino Francés, feature clear markings and a strong infrastructure of pilgrim hostels (albergues), eateries, and services designed for the needs of the pilgrim community, providing a reliable foundation for your experience.

- Rich Community Experience: Walking these pathways, like the millions who have gone before you, creates a sense of community and purpose. Connections that can last a lifetime are formed when pilgrims from all over the world meet and become close.

- Cultural and Historical Depth: Traditional paths are steeped in history and tradition, offering pilgrims the opportunity to explore the rich tapestry of the regions they travel through, including important religious and historical sites that enhance understanding and appreciation of the experience.

CONS:

- Crowding: Popular routes, such as the Camino Frances, can be crowded, especially during peak pilgrimage seasons, which can detract from the solitude and reflection that many seek. However, moments of quiet contemplation can still be found amidst the hustle and bustle.

- Predictability: Some may find that the well-established nature of these routes offers fewer opportunities for spontaneous exploration or discovery off the beaten path. Yet, even familiar paths can surprise you with their beauty and significance.

PERSONALIZED CAMINO

PROS:

- Flexibility: You can alter the daily walking distances, rest days, and exploration of less-traveled routes or areas of personal interest by personalizing your Camino. Those with certain physical demands or time limits will particularly value this versatility, which enables you to design an experience that genuinely speaks to you.

- Solitude: A personalized experience may provide more opportunities for solitude and introspection, away from the busier traditional routes. This can lead to a more introspective and personal pilgrimage that fosters deeper self-discovery.

- Unique Discoveries: Venturing off the traditional paths can lead to unexpected discoveries, from hidden natural wonders to small villages not typically experienced by the pilgrim masses. These unique experiences can enrich the pilgrimage in unforeseen ways, making your experience all the more special.

CONS:

- Logistical Challenges: Customizing your route requires more planning and research, particularly in securing accommodations and ensuring the availability of services along less-traveled paths. This can add a layer of complexity and uncertainty to your pilgrimage, but thorough preparation can lead to rewarding experiences.

- Reduced Support Network: Away from the main routes, the infrastructure and pilgrim support services may be less developed, necessitating greater self-reliance and preparation. Accepting this challenge can help you grow in confidence and independence.

- Potential Isolation: While solitude can be beneficial, it may also result in fewer opportunities to connect with fellow pilgrims. The communal aspect of the Camino, often cited as a highlight, may be less pronounced, but it opens up the possibility for profound personal reflection.

Analyze the benefits you want to get from your pilgrimage while choosing between a regular or customized Camino. The traditional routes offer a time-honored course if you're looking for an experience full of history, camaraderie, and a feeling of shared purpose. However, tailoring your itinerary might provide a more satisfying experience if your pilgrimage is focused on isolation, introspection, and the flexibility to go at your speed. The Camino de Santiago encourages pilgrims to explore not only the natural landscapes of Spain but also their internal landscapes, regardless of the route they take.

SOLO VS. GROUP TRAVEL CONSIDERATIONS

One important choice when walking the Camino de Santiago is whether to go alone or in a group. In terms of safety, flexibility, social connections, and decision-making, each option has pros and cons of its own. By assessing these elements, you can make sure that your trip is in line with your preferences and personal objectives, which will result in a rewarding experience.

For many pilgrims, safety is their top priority, especially those who are traveling alone and especially women traveling alone. Walking by yourself offers a great sensation of independence and privacy, which promotes reflection and a very intimate spiritual encounter. However, making this decision necessitates more personal security and awareness of one's surroundings. On the other hand, the presence of other people when traveling in a group automatically improves security. In an emergency, fellow pilgrims can provide prompt assistance and discourage possible safety hazards. Joining formal groups or making unofficial walking partners along the way can help lone travelers who are concerned about their safety strike a healthy balance between security and privacy.

Planning and daily decision-making flexibility differs significantly between solo and group travel. Pilgrims traveling alone have total freedom to choose their speed, stops, and itinerary, following their tastes or physical requirements. Those looking for a pilgrimage that is customized to meet their spiritual or personal development goals will find this degree of freedom appealing. However, group travel necessitates compromise and consensus, which might restrict spontaneity but also lessens the load of preparation and decision-making on one person. Groups can simplify logistical arrangements and even increase their cost-effectiveness by utilizing their common expertise and resources.

For many pilgrims, the social component of the Camino is particularly noteworthy. Meeting a wide variety of pilgrims on their own allows solo travelers to form relationships that can range from fleeting meetings to enduring friendships. For lone walkers, social connections frequently happen by chance, creating a diverse range of experiences. Although group travelers might be less receptive to outside interactions, they benefit from the support and camaraderie that their fellow passengers provide. The pilgrimage's emotional and spiritual impact might be increased by the group's shared experiences and recollections.

On the Camino, decisions range from routine logistical decisions to more profound, contemplative reflections on one's journey and mission. Traveling alone means that you are solely responsible for your choices, which can be both intimidating and liberating. A fully customized pilgrimage is made possible by the flexibility to select every element of the Camino experience, but it also necessitates independence and confidence. Travelers in groups benefit from deeper conversations and collective understanding as they share decision-making responsibilities. However, allowing for a range of viewpoints and preferences might occasionally result in concessions that might not suit everyone.

CHAPTER 4: GEAR UP FOR SUCCESS

LIGHTWEIGHT, SMART, AND PRACTICAL PACKING

A precise balance between minimalism and preparedness is necessary while packing for the Camino de Santiago. The secret is to choose multipurpose, lightweight, and intelligent goods so you only bring what you need. This methodical technique reduces the physical strain and streamlines your daily schedule so you can concentrate on the experience rather than taking care of your possessions.

Clothing

Choose clothing that dries quickly and can be layered with other clothing, adapting to changing weather conditions and temperatures. A base layer, mid-layer, and waterproof outer layer will be sufficient for most conditions. Opt for materials such as Merino wool or synthetic fibers that wick moisture away from the body. You can always wash and dry your clothes during your trip, so limit yourself to two or three clothing sets.

- Shirts: 2-3 lightweight, breathable tops
- Pants/Shorts: 1 pair of convertible pants and/or 1 pair of shorts
- Undergarments: 3-4 pairs of quick-dry underwear and socks
- Outerwear: 1 lightweight, waterproof jacket and 1 fleece or lightweight down jacket for cooler evenings
- Hat and Gloves: Depending on the season, a sun hat or a warm hat, along with a pair of gloves

Footwear

Your feet are your most valuable asset on the Camino. Invest in a pair of well-fitted, broken-in walking shoes or boots. Shoes should offer good support and breathability, with a waterproof coating for rainy days. Consider packing a pair of sandals or lightweight shoes for evenings to give your feet a well-deserved break.

Backpack

A lightweight, durable backpack with a capacity of 30-40 liters is ideal for most pilgrims. Look for a pack with a comfortable harness system, good weight distribution features, and enough pockets to keep your essentials accessible. A rain cover for your backpack is essential to protect your belongings.

Sleeping Gear

While many accommodations provide bedding, a lightweight sleeping bag liner or travel sheet adds warmth and ensures cleanliness. In warmer months, this may be all you need; in cooler seasons, a compact, lightweight sleeping bag rated to at least 40°F (4°C) provides extra comfort.

Toiletries and First Aid

Keep toiletries minimal: a small bottle of biodegradable soap serves as body wash, shampoo, and laundry detergent. Include a toothbrush, toothpaste, and a small quick-dry towel. Your first aid kit should contain blister care supplies, basic medications for pain and stomach upsets, and any personal medications.

Electronics and Miscellaneous

A smartphone can function as a camera, navigation tool, and communication device. Bring a portable charger and an international adapter. Other essentials include a water bottle, a knife or multi-tool (check airline regulations), and a lightweight journal or notebook for reflections.

Packing Tips

- Compression sacks reduce the volume of your clothing, making more room in your backpack.

- Pack heavier items closer to your back and higher up in your backpack for better weight distribution.

- Use packing cubes or Ziploc bags to organize items and keep them dry.

- Always place your rain gear and an extra layer in an easily accessible part of your backpack.

You may greatly lower the weight of your bag and improve your Camino experience by concentrating on the necessities and choosing multipurpose goods. The Camino is a route for spiritual development, cultural inquiry, and self-discovery. You may participate in every part of your pilgrimage with ease and confidence if you pack wisely.

SEASONAL PACKING ESSENTIALS

Preparing for the Camino de Santiago requires careful planning, especially regarding packing for the various climates you might face. Comfort and safety depend on recognizing the seasonal differences along your chosen route and selecting gear that can adapt to these changes. This guide outlines essential packing strategies for each season, ensuring you are well-equipped for your pilgrimage.

Spring (March to May)

Spring on the Camino can be unpredictable, with both warm days and chilly mornings or evenings. Rain is also a common phenomenon.

- Clothing: Layering proves crucial. Start with a moisture-wicking base layer, add a warm mid-layer like a lightweight fleece, and finish with a waterproof and windproof jacket. Choose breathable, quick-dry pants, and consider layering thermal leggings underneath during colder mornings.
- Rain Gear: A durable, lightweight rain jacket and waterproof pants are essential. A waterproof backpack cover and a small, quick-dry towel for wiping down wet surfaces or gear are also advisable.
- Accessories: Waterproof gloves and a warm hat for cold mornings, along with a sun hat for brighter days. Sunglasses and sunscreen are necessary as the days grow longer.

Summer (June to August)

Although temperatures rise in the summer, heat waves can occasionally happen. Making sun protection and water a priority becomes crucial.

- Clothing: Choose lightweight, breathable fabrics. Loose-fitting, long-sleeved shirts provide sun protection while keeping you cool. Select shorts or convertible pants for versatility. A light, breathable hat with a brim offers sun protection.
- Rain Gear: Although less common, summer storms can happen, so pack a lightweight rain jacket and consider a rain cover for your backpack.
- Accessories: High-SPF sunscreen, UV-protection sunglasses, and a lightweight scarf or bandana to protect your neck from the sun. A reusable water bottle with a wide mouth for easy refilling is crucial to staying hydrated.

Fall (September to November)

Autumn brings cooler temperatures and increased rainfall, especially in the later months. The landscape is stunning, but preparation for variable weather is key.

- Clothing: Reintroduce layers with a focus on warmth and moisture management. A waterproof and windproof jacket remains essential, paired with mid-layers that can be easily added or removed. Convertible pants offer flexibility for changing temperatures.
- Rain Gear: Reliable rainwear is crucial as showers become more frequent. Ensure your footwear is waterproof and consider gaiters to keep mud and water out of your boots.
- Accessories: Warm gloves, a beanie for cooler days, and a lightweight hat for sunnier weather. A headlamp may become more useful as the days shorten.

Winter (December to February)

Winter on the Camino can be challenging, with cold temperatures, snow, and rain. Fewer pilgrims tackle the Camino in winter, but those who do will find a unique solitude and beauty.

- Clothing: Thermal base layers are essential for retaining body heat. Add a heavyweight fleece or down jacket for insulation and ensure your outer layer is both waterproof and insulated. Waterproof pants are also recommended.
- Rain Gear: A high-quality, insulated rain jacket and pants are necessary to protect against snow and rain. Waterproof boots with a good grip are essential to navigate slippery paths.
- Accessories: Insulated gloves, a warm hat that covers the ears, and thermal socks are must-haves. Consider snow gaiters for deeper snow conditions. A thermal flask to keep liquids warm can be a comforting addition.

General Tips Across All Seasons:

- Footwear: Regardless of the season, your shoes should be well broken-in, offering good support and breathability, with a waterproof coating for wet conditions.
- Backpack: A 30-40 liter backpack fitted with a rain cover should suffice for carrying your essentials. Ensure it has a comfortable harness and adequate pockets for easy access to gear.
- Packing Strategy: Organize and minimize the volume of your clothing using compression sacks and packing cubes. Keep essentials like rain gear and an extra layer easily accessible.

Tailoring your packing list to the season of your Camino experience ensures a more comfortable and enjoyable time. The Camino presents not just a physical challenge but also opportunities for self-discovery and spiritual growth. Being well-prepared allows you to focus on the transformative aspects of your pilgrimage, appreciating each moment with confidence and ease.

BACKPACK, FOOTWEAR, AND GEAR

Selecting the right backpack, footwear, and gear plays a vital role in ensuring a comfortable and injury-free Camino experience. These items serve as your primary tools on the pilgrimage, directly affecting your comfort, performance, and overall enjoyment. Let's break down how to choose each piece with precision.

Backpack

A well-fitted backpack serves as the cornerstone of your gear. Aim for a 30-40 liter capacity, which provides ample space for essentials while discouraging overpacking. Key features to look for include:

- Adjustable Straps: Choose a backpack with adjustable shoulder, chest, and waist straps to distribute weight evenly across your body.

- Ventilation: A mesh back panel promotes airflow, reducing sweat and discomfort during long walks.

- Pockets and Compartments: Multiple pockets help organize gear for easy access. A dedicated compartment for a hydration system can be a game changer.

- Rain Cover: This feature protects your belongings during unexpected downpours.

Footwear

Your choice of footwear can significantly influence your Camino experience. Prioritize comfort and durability. Whether you opt for walking shoes or boots, consider the following:

- Fit: Footwear should feel snug but not tight, allowing enough room to wiggle your toes. Keep in mind that feet swell during long walks, so trying shoes a half size larger than usual can make a significant difference.

- Support: Look for shoes that provide good arch support and a cushioned sole to absorb impact.

- Breathability: Materials like Gore-Tex allow your feet to breathe while keeping them dry in wet conditions.

- Traction: Durable soles with deep lugs offer better grip on varied terrains.

- Break-in Period: Wear your shoes on several long walks before the Camino to prevent blisters and discomfort.

Essential Gear

Beyond your backpack and shoes, several key items will enhance your Camino experience:

- Walking Poles: These reduce strain on knees and ankles, especially during descents. Choose lightweight, adjustable poles with comfortable grips.

- Hydration System: A water bladder or durable water bottles ensure you stay hydrated without constantly stopping to drink.

- Headlamp: For early starts or late finishes, a headlamp is essential for safety.

- Multi-tool: A compact multi-tool proves invaluable for minor repairs, adjustments, or preparing snacks.

- Blister Kit: Include adhesive bandages, antiseptic wipes, and blister pads to manage foot care on the go.

- Sun Protection: A hat, sunglasses, and sunscreen are essential for protecting against sun exposure.

Packing Strategy

- Weight Distribution: Pack heavier items closer to your back and higher up for better balance.

- Accessibility: Keep frequently used items like water, snacks, and your rain jacket in easily accessible pockets.

- Compression Sacks: Use these to minimize the volume of your clothing, creating more space for other essentials.

A strong foundation for a successful pilgrimage is created by carefully choosing and testing your footwear, bag, and other equipment before the Camino. The proper gear allows you to fully participate in the life-changing Camino de Santiago experience by improving your physical comfort and promoting your mental and spiritual health.

CHAPTER 5: TRAINING FOR THE TRAIL

• • • • •

PREPARING YOUR BODY AND MIND

Walking the Camino de Santiago represents more than a physical challenge; it involves a deep commitment of both body and mind. Comprehensive preparation is essential to walk this pilgrimage with resilience and mindfulness. This preparation goes beyond physical preparation and includes mental strength, emotional resilience, and spiritual openness, all of which are vital for a transformative experience on the Camino.

Physical preparation is the foundation of your Camino experience. Begin training at least six months before your departure to gradually increase your endurance and prepare your body for the long distances you will cover each day. Start with shorter hikes, progressively increasing the distance and incorporating varied terrain to mimic the conditions of the Camino. This gradual approach improves your physical endurance and reduces the risk of injury. Do cardiovascular exercises, such as cycling or swimming, to further improve your endurance, and includestrength training for your legs, back, and core to provide the muscle support needed to carry your backpack over long distances.

Setting specific goals for your journey is frequently the first step in mental preparation, which is equally important. Think about the things you want to learn or accomplish while walking the Camino, whether it's healing, personal development, spiritual enlightenment, or just the challenge of finishing the journey. Understanding your driving forces will help you stay focused and resilient in trying times. Having a clear purpose can be a great ally.

Meditation and mindfulness exercises can help you develop mental resilience, and they are great resources for the Camino. These exercises educate you to be in the present, observe without passing judgment, and enjoy every moment with openness and thankfulness. To develop a mindset that will help you with the emotional and physical highs and lows of the pilgrimage, incorporate brief meditation sessions into your daily schedule. A satisfying Camino experience depends on your ability to pay attention to your body and mind, knowing when to exert yourself and when to take breaks.

Emotional preparation involves anticipating and accepting the wide range of feelings that the Camino will evoke. The experience encompasses both inward exploration and outward challenges. Pilgrims often encounter moments of profound joy, serenity, and connection alongside feelings of loneliness, frustration, and physical discomfort. You may handle these feelings with poise and fortitude if you recognize and embrace them as a natural part of the experience. Along the process, embracing this range of emotions can result in more profound understandings and relationships.

Spiritual preparation may not resonate with everyone, but for many, the Camino offers a deeply spiritual experience. Regardless of your religious beliefs, being open to the spiritual dimensions of the Camino can enrich your journey. Engage with the historical and religious significance of the sites you visit, participate in pilgrim rituals, or remain open to moments of reflection and connection throughout the experience.

Preparing your body and mind for the Camino de Santiago requires a comprehensive approach that addresses physical fitness, mental resilience, emotional preparation, and spiritual opening. Dedicating time and effort to each of these aspects equips you not just to walk the Camino but to embrace its transformative potential, making every step a move toward growth, understanding, and fulfillment. This holistic preparation allows you to approach your pilgrimage with confidence, purpose, and an open heart, ready to receive the countless gifts that the Camino has to offer.

REALISTIC PLANS TO BUILD STAMINA

Building stamina for the Camino de Santiago requires dedication, consistency, and a tailored approach to fit your current fitness level. Whether you are a beginner or have a moderate level of fitness, enhancing your endurance, strength, and mental resilience is essential for handling long distances day after day. The following plans cater to different starting points and focus on walking routines and strength exercises that prepare your body for the challenges ahead.

For Beginners: Building a Foundation

Starting from a low fitness level demands a measured approach to avoid injury while gradually increasing stamina. Walk 2-3 times a week, aiming for 30 minutes per session. Each week, add 5-10 minutes to your walking time until you can comfortably walk for 60 minutes. Include varied terrain in your walks, such as hills or trails, to simulate the conditions of the Camino. This practice builds physical endurance and helps you mentally prepare for the changing landscapes you will encounter.

Strength training is equally important, as it focuses on the leg, core, and back muscles that will support you throughout your pilgrimage. Begin with simple bodyweight exercises twice a week, including squats, lunges, planks, and back extensions. Perform 2-3 sets of 10-12 repetitions for each exercise, ensuring proper form to prevent injuries. As your fitness improves, gradually increase the intensity by adding more repetitions and sets or incorporating weights.

For Intermediate Walkers: Enhancing Endurance and Strength

Those with a moderate level of fitness should aim to walk 4-5 times a week, including at least one long walk (90 minutes to 2 hours) in their routine. This approach helps your body adapt to longer periods of physical activity, which is crucial for the daily distances on the Camino. Include back-to-back walking days to simulate consecutive walking days on the trail, allowing your body to adjust to the recovery needs.

Focus on strength training exercises that enhance endurance and stability. Incorporate weighted squats, deadlifts, and lunges into your routine, along with core-strengthening exercises like Russian twists and leg raises. Try to do 3 sets of 12-15 repetitions, emphasizing endurance over high resistance. Adding balance exercises, such as single-leg stands or using a balance board, improves stability and reduces the risk of falls or ankle sprains on uneven terrain.

Cross-Training for All Levels

Cross-training plays a crucial role in preventing overuse injuries and improving overall fitness. Activities such as cycling, swimming, or yoga complement your walking and strength training by enhancing cardiovascular health, flexibility, and mental well-being. Include at least one day of cross-training per week, selecting activities you enjoy that provide a good balance to your walking routine.

Consistency and Recovery

Consistency is necessary to increase endurance, but recovery is equally important. Schedule at least one rest day per week to allow your body to recover and repair. Pay attention to your body; if you experience excessive fatigue or soreness, take additional rest days. Proper nutrition, hydration, and sleep are vital components of your training plan, as they support your body's needs during increased physical activity.

Mental Preparation

Stamina involves both physical and mental aspects; mental resilience significantly influences long-distance walking. Incorporate mindfulness or meditation into your routine, focusing on cultivating a positive mindset and visualizing your success on the Camino. This mental preparation is as crucial as the physical one, enabling you to tackle challenges with confidence and determination.

Following these realistic plans and adjusting them based on your progress will help you build the stamina, strength, and mental resilience required for a successful and fulfilling Camino de Santiago experience. Preparing your body and mind is essential for the pilgrimage, laying the groundwork for a transformative experience.

Preventing Injuries and Staying Strong

Injury prevention plays a crucial role in preparing for the Camino de Santiago. Effective strategies allow pilgrims to significantly reduce the risk of common injuries linked to long-distance walking. This section highlights essential practices such as stretching, hydration, foot care, and recovery techniques to help you stay strong and capable throughout your time on the Camino.

Stretching

Regularly stretching your muscles is vital for preventing strains and enhancing flexibility, which reduces the likelihood of injuries. Focus on dynamic stretches before walking to prepare your muscles for the activity ahead. Include leg swings, arm circles, and gentle lunges in your routine. After your walk, engage in static stretching to help your muscles relax and recover. Target key areas such as the calves, hamstrings, quadriceps, and lower back. Hold each stretch for at least 30 seconds to encourage optimal muscle elongation and flexibility, allowing for freer movement.

Hydration

Maintaining hydration is crucial for supporting muscle function and preventing cramps, a common issue for pilgrims. Aim to drink at least half an ounce to an ounce of water for each pound you weigh daily. Increase this amount with exertion and exposure to heat. Carry a reusable water bottle and refill it at available water stations along the Camino. Consider using electrolyte supplements or drinks to maintain the balance of minerals in your body, especially during longer walking days or in hot weather, which helps keep your energy levels up.

Foot Care

Proper foot care stands out as the most important injury prevention strategy for the Camino. Start with well-fitting, used footwear to minimize the risk of blisters. Apply blister-preventative tape or plasters to known hot spots before they develop into blisters. Keep your feet dry and clean by changing socks at least once during the day to prevent moisture buildup. At the end of each day, wash your feet, dry them thoroughly, and apply moisturizer to prevent cracking. If a blister forms, clean the area gently, sterilize a needle, and drain the blister without removing the skin. Cover it with a sterile dressing to protect against infection, allowing you to stay focused on your path.

Adequate recovery sustains your strength throughout the pilgrimage. Incorporate rest days into your walking schedule, especially after particularly long or strenuous segments. Use compression garments to improve circulation and reduce muscle soreness. Engage in light, restorative activities on rest days, such as gentle yoga or swimming, to aid muscle recovery without overexertion. Nutrition plays a key role in recovery; prioritize a balanced diet rich in proteins, carbohydrates, and healthy fats to repair and fuel your body. Another essential element is sleep, which enables your body to recover and regenerate. To promote your general well-being, try to get 7 to 9 hours of good sleep every night and, if necessary, take quick naps during the day.

Your physical resilience will increase if you incorporate these injury prevention and recovery techniques into your daily routine and Camino preparation. This preventative measure lowers your chance of suffering from common walking-related injuries and guarantees that you may participate completely in the Camino de Santiago's life-changing experience on a physical and spiritual level. It is still crucial to pay attention to your body and meet its requirements because taking good care of it will help you walk the Camino with confidence.

PART II: CAMINO ROUTES

The Camino de Santiago, a network of ancient pilgrim routes that stretch across Europe and converge at the tomb of St. James in northwestern Spain, captivates the hearts of many. This pilgrimage offers a unique blend of physical challenge, spiritual enrichment, and cultural immersion. Each route possesses its own appeal, challenges, and historical significance. A detailed understanding of these routes is crucial for planning a pilgrimage that aligns with your personal goals, fitness level, and interests.

The Camino Francés, often regarded as the most traditional path, spans approximately 780 kilometers from Saint-Jean-Pied-de-Port in France to Santiago de Compostela in Spain. It is well-known for its established infrastructure, vibrant pilgrim community, and rich cultural landmarks. This route suits those seeking a classic Camino experience, providing opportunities to engage deeply with fellow pilgrims and connect with the communal spirit of the path.

The Camino Portugués presents two distinct paths: the Central Route and the Coastal Route. The Central Route, which begins in Lisbon or Porto in Portugal, showcases historical cities, rolling vineyards, and the serene beauty of the Portuguese countryside. In contrast, the Coastal Route, also starting in Porto, follows the Atlantic coastline, offering breathtaking ocean views and a chance to explore the unique maritime culture of northern Portugal and Galicia. Both routes combine natural beauty and cultural richness, making the Camino Portugués a versatile choice for pilgrims.

The Camino del Norte takes a northern passage across Spain, following the rugged coastlines of the Basque Country, Cantabria, Asturias, and Galicia. This route takes you through northern Spain's lush landscapes, isolated beaches, and breathtaking coastline views. It remains less traveled, providing a sense of solitude and reflection for those who choose its winding trails. The Camino del Norte attracts adventurers and those seeking a path away from the more crowded routes.

The Camino Primitivo, known as the Original Way, represents the oldest route to Santiago, predating even the Camino Francés. It begins in Oviedo and is famous for its challenging mountainous terrain, remote wilderness, and the profound sense of history that permeates its ancient paths. This route suits those looking for a physically demanding experience intertwined with deep historical and spiritual resonance.

Each of these routes presents unique challenges and rewards, satisfying a broad spectrum of tastes and demands. Whether you are drawn to the camaraderie and rich historical tapestry of the Camino Francés, the scenic diversity of the Camino Portugués, the rugged beauty of the Camino del Norte, or the ancient and challenging paths of the Camino Primitivo, your experience will undoubtedly be transformative. Exploring the specifics of each route, including terrain, key stops, and practical tips for pilgrims, reveals that the Camino de Santiago serves as a profound experience that touches the soul.

The Camino Inglés serves as an excellent introduction to the Camino experience for beginners or those with limited time. This route extends over a relatively short distance from Ferrol or A Coruña to Santiago, offering a blend of coastal scenery, historical sites, and a quieter walking experience. It makes for a perfect choice for reflection and a more intimate pilgrimage. The shorter length enhances the rich cultural and spiritual experiences it provides, creating a rewarding opportunity for those seeking the essence of the Camino in a condensed format. Discover and connect with what lies ahead.

The Via de la Plata begins in Seville and stretches northward through the heart of Spain to Santiago, making it the longest Camino route steeped in history and following ancient Roman roads. This path presents a unique experience through the diverse landscapes and cultural heritage of western Spain, from the vibrant cities of Andalusia to the tranquil countryside of Castile and León and finally into the lush regions of Galicia. Its length and relative solitude attract those looking for a challenge while allowing for deep immersion in Spain's rich history and varied landscapes. Take each step with intention, and you'll uncover the beauty along the way.

Pilgrims who feel called to continue beyond Santiago can explore the extension to Finisterre and Muxía. Walking to Finisterre, once believed to be the end of the known world, and then on to the rugged coast of Muxía offers a powerful conclusion to the pilgrimage. This path encourages reflection at the ocean's edge, where many participate in the ritual of watching the sunset over the water, symbolizing the completion of a transformative experience. These less-frequented routes provide tranquility, breathtaking ocean views, and a chance to engage with local traditions and the spiritual significance of reaching what was once considered the edge of the world. Let this experience enhance your understanding of your path.

Several other paths, such as the Camino de Invierno and the Camino de Madrid, present alternative experiences for those seeking different perspectives or starting points within Spain. Each route, with its distinct characteristics, challenges, and rewards, contributes to the rich tapestry of the Camino de Santiago pilgrimage. Personal objectives, physical capabilities, and the desire for historical, cultural, or environmental experiences should all be taken into consideration when choosing a route. Whatever route is taken, the trip to Santiago promotes spiritual rejuvenation, community, and self-discovery. Every action ends in development. The Camino de Santiago, with its countless routes, offers a unique experience to each pilgrim. Whether seeking solitude, adventure, cultural immersion, or spiritual enlightenment, the Camino provides a backdrop for personal transformations. The preparation, challenges, and reflections along the way contribute to a profound sense of accomplishment and personal growth. Pilgrims walk through these ancient paths.

Pilgrims walk through these ancient paths, joining a community of millions who have walked before them, each adding their own story to the ongoing legacy of the Camino de Santiago. Your experience becomes part of something much larger, a beautiful story waiting to unfold.

CHAPTER 6: CAMINO FRANCÉS

MOST POPULAR ROUTE: HISTORICAL SIGNIFICANCE

The Camino Francés owes its popularity to its historical significance and the well-established infrastructure alongside the vibrant community of pilgrims it attracts. This route, trodden by millions over centuries, serves as the backbone of the Camino de Santiago pilgrimage, deeply embedded

The Camino Francés owes its popularity to its historical significance and the well-established infrastructure alongside the vibrant community of pilgrims it attracts. This route, trodden by millions over centuries, serves as the backbone of the Camino de Santiago pilgrimage, deeply embedded in the cultural and spiritual fabric of Europe. The historical significance of the Camino Francés is immense, tracing back to the early 9th century when the remains of Saint James were purportedly discovered in Santiago de Compostela. This discovery transformed the city into a major pilgrimage site, with the Camino Francés becoming the most favored route due to its relative safety and the hospitality provided by monasteries along the way. Over time, kings, nobles, and commoners alike have traveled this path, each contributing to the route's rich tapestry of history and tradition.

The infrastructure of the Camino Francés stands out among the various Camino routes. It features a comprehensive network of albergues (pilgrim hostels), restaurants, and services specifically designed to meet the needs of modern pilgrims. This infrastructure has evolved to support the physical and spiritual aspects of the pilgrimage, offering a blend of comfort and challenge that enriches the overall experience. Well-marked trails and pilgrim-focused medical services ensure that every aspect of the Camino Francés prioritizes the welfare of the pilgrims. This level of support eases the logistical concerns of travelers and fosters a sense of safety and community, creating an environment where every step feels manageable.

The sense of community on the Camino Frances is its main attraction. The route is renowned for the camaraderie that develops among pilgrims, a diverse but like-minded group of people from all corners of the world. This community spirit becomes evident from the very start in Saint-Jean-Pied-de-Port, where many pilgrims begin their travels. Walking, eating, and lodging in albergues together create relationships that frequently endure a lifetime. The route facilitates a unique social environment where conversations flow freely, stories are exchanged, and support is offered without hesitation. This strong sense of belonging and mutual understanding among pilgrims enhances the transformative nature of the pilgrimage, making the Camino Francés not just a physical endeavor but a profoundly social and spiritual experience as well.

The Camino Francés also celebrates its cultural richness, offering pilgrims a tapestry of experiences that span the breadth of Spanish history, art, and tradition. The majestic cathedrals and historic cities like Pamplona, Burgos, and León, along with the serene beauty of the Meseta and the lush landscapes of Galicia, create a continuous exploration of time and tradition. Each step along the Camino Francés presents an opportunity to immerse oneself in the local culture, sample regional cuisines, and participate in age-old traditions, further enriching the pilgrim's experience and encouraging personal reflection.

The Camino Francés stands out as the most popular route to Santiago de Compostela due to its deep historical roots, comprehensive infrastructure, and the vibrant community of pilgrims it attracts. It is an unmatched option for individuals looking for a life-changing pilgrimage experience because of its unique fusion of cultural diversity, historical significance, and community spirit. This route offers stunning landscapes of northern Spain alongside opportunities for personal growth, reflection, and connection with fellow travelers. These qualities continue to draw pilgrims to this ancient path, seeking both the challenge of the walk and the promise of spiritual renewal.

TERRAIN, STOPS, AND SECRETS

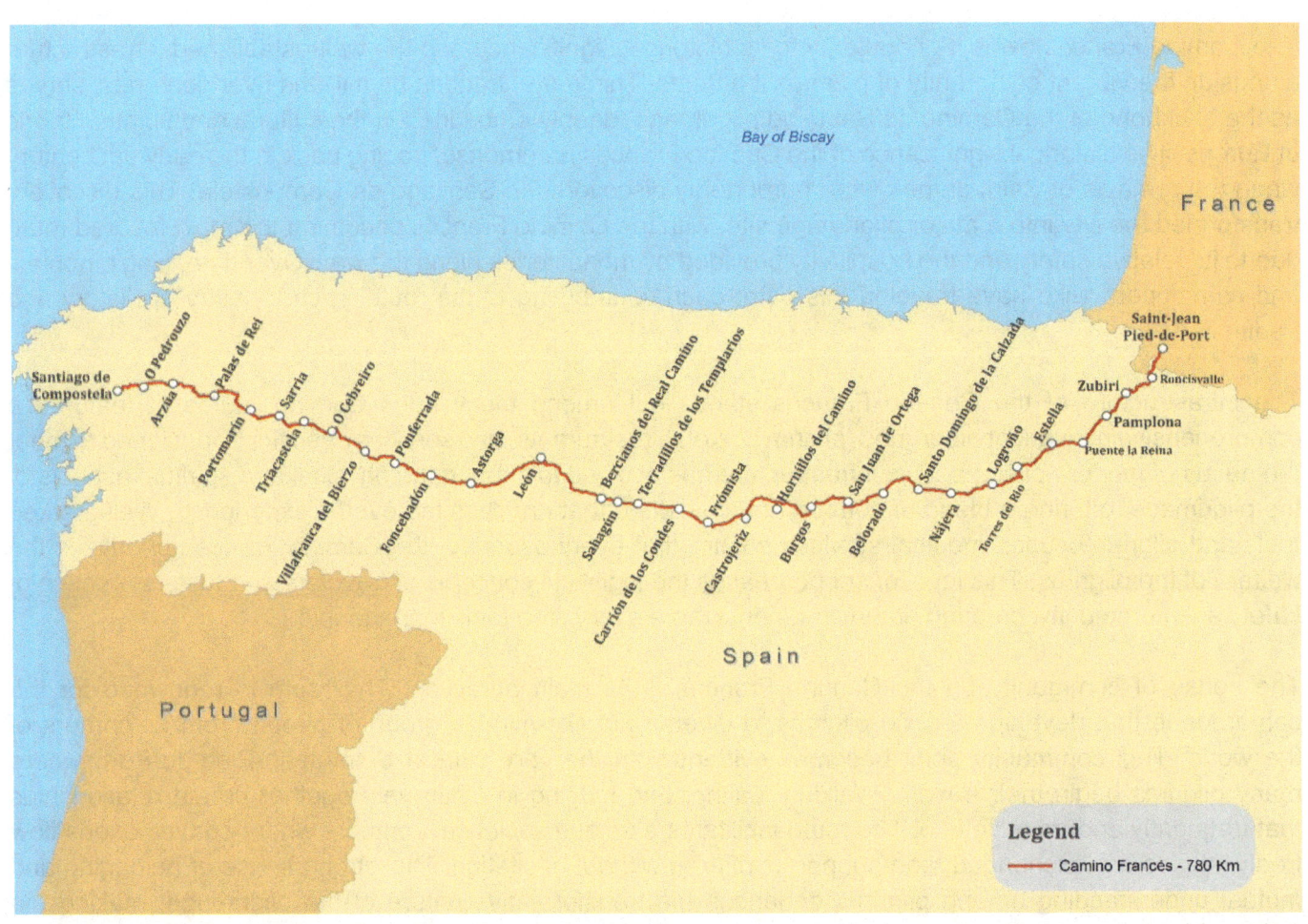

Km (15.5 miles) | 6 to 8 hours | Difficult

The Camino Frances starts in Saint-Jean-Pied-de-Port and includes a strenuous but worthwhile journey over the Pyrenees. Given the breathtaking mountain vistas that signal the actual start of their journey, many pilgrims find this first stretch to be both physically taxing and spiritually cleansing. The famous statue of the Virgin Mary at Orisson, which provides visitors with a moment of protection and contemplation, and the old Roncesvalles Monastery, a well-known resting area for pilgrims seeking rejuvenation before continuing, are noteworthy stops along the route.

The Camino experiences a significant change in scenery as it crosses the Meseta and travels across expansive, open plains. This section takes roughly 8 to 10 hours to complete and spans about 40 kilometers (24.8 miles). This stage tests the pilgrims' endurance and mental fortitude rather than their physical strength because it has long, straight routes and little shade. The uncomplicated landscape promotes introspection and stops along the journey. For example, León's magnificent stained-glass cathedral and historic Roman walls are places of reflection.

40 km (24.8 miles) | 8 to 10 hours | Difficult

As the route moves into the heart of Navarre and La Rioja, the rugged mountain terrain gives way to rolling hills, vineyards, and medieval villages. This section, spanning roughly 22 kilometers (13.7 miles) and taking around 5 to 7 hours to walk, is less physically demanding, allowing for a more relaxed, contemplative experience. Key highlights include the town of Estella, home to the impressive Church of San Pedro de la Rúa, and the famous wine fountain at Irache, where pilgrims can enjoy a taste of local tradition. The journey through Burgos brings another major highlight—the city's stunning Gothic cathedral, a masterpiece of Spanish architecture that invites visitors to explore its deep historical and artistic heritage.

22 km (13.7 miles) | 5 to 7 hours | Easy

The landscape gradually shifts again to undulating hills as the Camino passes through the province of León and into Galicia, leading to the ascent to O Cebreiro. The entrance to the verdant Galician countryside, which is dotted with eucalyptus forests and frequently experiences misty rains, is marked by this small settlement, which is well-known for its Celtic heritage. This stretch, about 28 kilometers (17.4 miles) long and taking 7 to 9 hours to complete, introduces pilgrims to Galicia's unique character, from the region's distinctive thatched-roof stone houses (pallozas) to the enduring legends of miracles and hospitality, such as the famed Santo Milagro at the Church of Santa María la Real.

Galicia itself is a mystical and vibrant region, where the Camino winds through ancient woodlands, past streams and into villages filled with the scent of eucalyptus and the sound of traditional Galician bagpipes. Sarria, a bustling town, serves as a popular starting point for many pilgrims, as it sits just over the 100-kilometer minimum required to receive the Compostela. From here, the final stretch is dotted with small hamlets, each with its unique charm, such as the century-old eucalyptus tree near Portomarín or the Romanesque Church of Vilar de Donas, once guarded by the Knights of Santiago.

28 kilometers (17.4 miles) | 7 to 9 hours | Easy

The last leg to Santiago de Compostela builds anticipation and reflection. At Monte do Gozo, pilgrims catch their first glimpse of the cathedral's towering spires—a moment that often brings an overwhelming sense of accomplishment and emotion. Stepping into Santiago, the journey's final steps are filled with relief, joy, and deep contemplation. The walk culminates in the grand Praza do Obradoiro, where the magnificent Cathedral of Santiago marks not just the end of a long physical journey but the beginning of a new personal and spiritual understanding.

Throughout the Camino Francés, the terrain itself becomes part of the pilgrim's experience—both a physical challenge and a backdrop for personal transformation. Every stretch of the route, from rugged mountains to endless plains and misty forests, weaves together the rich cultural and historical heritage of Spain with the deeply personal reflections of each traveler. The well-maintained infrastructure—marked trails, pilgrim hostels, and warm local hospitality—ensures that those who embark on this path are supported every step of the way. With its ever-changing landscapes, historical depth, and powerful sense of community, the Camino Francés remains a testament to the timeless appeal of the pilgrimage to Santiago de Compostela.

Landmarks and Insider Tips

Beyond the well-trodden path of the Camino Francés lie hidden gems and insider tips that can truly transform your pilgrimage into an unforgettable experience. Taking a tiny detour from the main path might provide discoveries that enhance your understanding of the local history, culture, and food. Here are some must-see places, suggestions for regional cuisine, and professional advice for the best Camino Francés experience.

Hidden Gems:

- Viana: Just before reaching Logroño, the town of Viana offers a captivating glimpse into the past with its charming old town and the Church of Santa María. This lesser-known stop is perfect for exploring without the crowds, allowing you to savor the full essence of this beautiful area.

- San Juan de Ortega: Nestled between Burgos and Atapuerca, this tiny hamlet is home to a monastery with a remarkable Romanesque church. It serves as a place of serenity and spiritual reflection, providing a peaceful retreat away from the busier stops.

- O Cebreiro: While not entirely off the beaten path, the village of O Cebreiro feels like stepping back in time. Its traditional pallozas and the panoramic views of the surrounding mountains offer a unique experience that invites you to pause and appreciate the beauty around you.

Local Food Recommendations:

- Pulpo a la Gallega: In Melide, try this traditional Galician octopus dish. Tender and flavorful, it stands out as a culinary highlight of the region that will surely delight your taste buds.

- Tarta de Santiago: This almond cake, often dusted with powdered sugar and marked with the Cross of Saint James, is a must-try sweet treat available throughout Galicia, adding a touch of sweetness to your experience.
- Rioja Wine: The Camino Francés passes through the renowned Rioja wine region. Visit a local bodega for a tasting session to savor the local vintages and immerse yourself in the regional culture.

Insider Tips:

Early Starts: Begin your day's walk before sunrise to enjoy the tranquility of the Camino and avoid the midday heat. This approach ensures you arrive early at your next stop, securing accommodation in the more popular towns, which sets you up for a more relaxed experience.

Carry a Credential Stamp Book: Get your pilgrim passport stamped at each stop. This step is necessary for obtaining the Compostela certificate and becomes a cherished memento of your experience, reminding you of the steps you've taken.

Engage with Locals: Take the time to speak with residents and fellow pilgrims. These interactions can lead to recommendations for must-visit spots and eateries that aren't in guidebooks, enriching your experience with local insights.

Attend a Pilgrim Mass: Whether you hold religious beliefs or not, attending a pilgrim mass in towns like Santiago de Compostela can be a moving experience, offering a sense of camaraderie and closure that resonates long after.

Pack Lightly but Wisely: Remember that every extra pound in your backpack will be felt over the miles. Pack only the essentials while including layers for changing weather conditions and a small first aid kit, ensuring you're prepared for whatever comes your way.

tay Hydrated and Protected: The Spanish sun can be intense, especially on the Meseta. Carry a refillable water bottle and sunscreen to protect yourself from the elements and maintain your energy as you walk.

Including these sites, regional cuisine, and insider knowledge in your Camino Francés journey can enhance it with life-changing experiences that extend beyond the actual trek. The Camino presents a special chance for introspection, personal development, and reconnection with the outside world. If you give it your all, you'll find that the real charm of the Camino is in the unexpected encounters and the hidden gems you find along the route.

ALTERNATIVE ROUTES TO SANTIAGO

While the Camino Francés is the most popular route, several alternative paths offer unique experiences, allowing pilgrims to explore quieter trails while immersing themselves in local history, culture, and landscapes. These lesser-known routes not only provide a more intimate journey but also introduce a deeper connection with the traditions of the regions they pass through. Below, we explore three noteworthy alternatives: the Camino Aragonés, the Camino del Ebro, and the Ruta de la Lana.

Camino Aragonés

170 kilometers (105 miles) | 7 to 9 days | Difficult

The Camino Aragonés serves as a connecting route between the Camino Francés and the Camino del Norte, spanning approximately 170 kilometers (105 miles). It is usually finished in 7 to 9 days by pilgrims, who travel through a landscape that alternates between undulating hills and more mountainous areas. This moderately challenging route rewards travelers with stunning views and a quieter, more reflective experience.

Along the way, Jaca stands out as a key stop, home to an impressive Romanesque cathedral that reflects the region's medieval heritage. Another highlight is Puente la Reina de Jaca, famous for its centuries-old stone bridge, a reminder of the many pilgrims who have crossed it before. These towns offer not just rest but also opportunities to experience local culture, savor regional cuisine, and connect with fellow travelers.

The Pyrenees provide a breathtaking backdrop, creating a sense of wonder and reflection as you make your way through remote villages and open landscapes. Unlike the busier Camino Francés, this route allows for a more peaceful journey, where solitude fosters introspection and a deeper appreciation of nature.

For those seeking both a physical challenge and a spiritual retreat, the Camino Aragonés is an excellent choice, blending history, culture, and natural beauty into an enriching pilgrimage experience.

Camino del Ebro

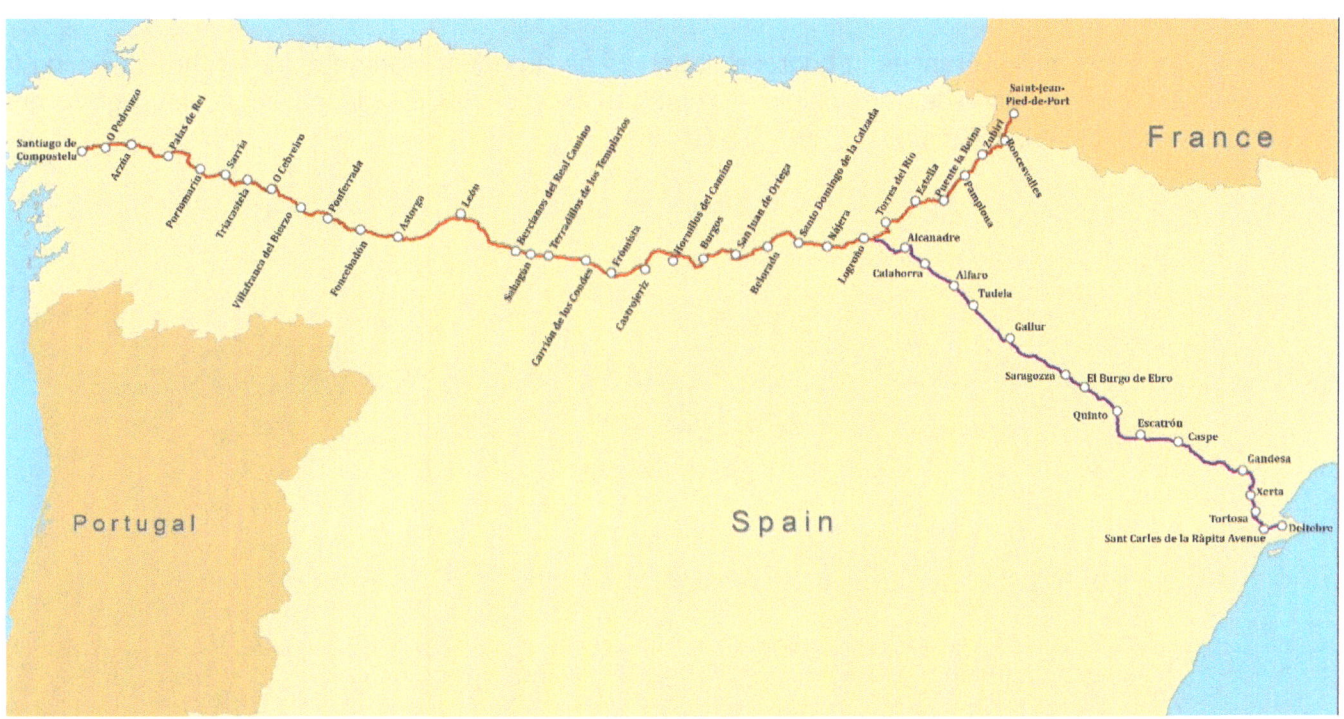

452 kilometers (280 miles) | 18 to 21 days | Difficult

The Camino del Ebro is a captivating alternative route that follows the course of the Ebro River, Spain's longest waterway, offering pilgrims a unique blend of natural beauty, cultural heritage, and historical significance. Spanning approximately 452 kilometers (280 miles) from Deltebre on the Mediterranean coast to Logroño, where it connects with the Camino Francés, this route takes around 18 to 21 days to complete, depending on one's pace.

Unlike the more traditional mountainous or rural Caminos, the Camino del Ebro is characterized by its relatively flat terrain, making it an accessible choice for walkers of all fitness levels. Its paths meander through vineyards, orchards, fertile plains, and historic towns, providing a peaceful and contemplative pilgrimage experience.

One of the major highlights of this route is Zaragoza, the capital of Aragón, home to the stunning Basilica del Pilar, one of Spain's most revered pilgrimage sites. Pilgrims passing through can admire its magnificent Baroque architecture and take a moment of reflection in its sacred halls.

Further along, the Rioja wine region welcomes travelers with its renowned vineyards and charming towns. Logroño, a major stop along the route, is famous for its tapas culture and world-class wines. Here, pilgrims can indulge in the rich culinary traditions of La Rioja, enjoying a well-deserved moment of relaxation before continuing their journey.

The route also passes through Alfaro, a town known for its majestic Colegiata de San Miguel, a historic basilica that offers a tranquil space for contemplation. The rhythmic flow of the Ebro River accompanies the journey, reinforcing the reflective and meditative quality of the walk.

For those looking to experience a Camino that blends history, gastronomy, and nature, the Camino del Ebro provides a rewarding alternative to the more well-known routes. Whether drawn by the cultural richness of its cities, the scenic landscapes along the river, or the opportunity to explore Spain's viticultural traditions, this route offers a diverse and enriching pilgrimage experience.

Connecting with the Camino Francés in Logroño, it serves as a perfect starting point for those wishing to extend their journey to Santiago de Compostela, making it an excellent choice for both seasoned pilgrims and those embarking on their first Camino.

Ruta de la Lana

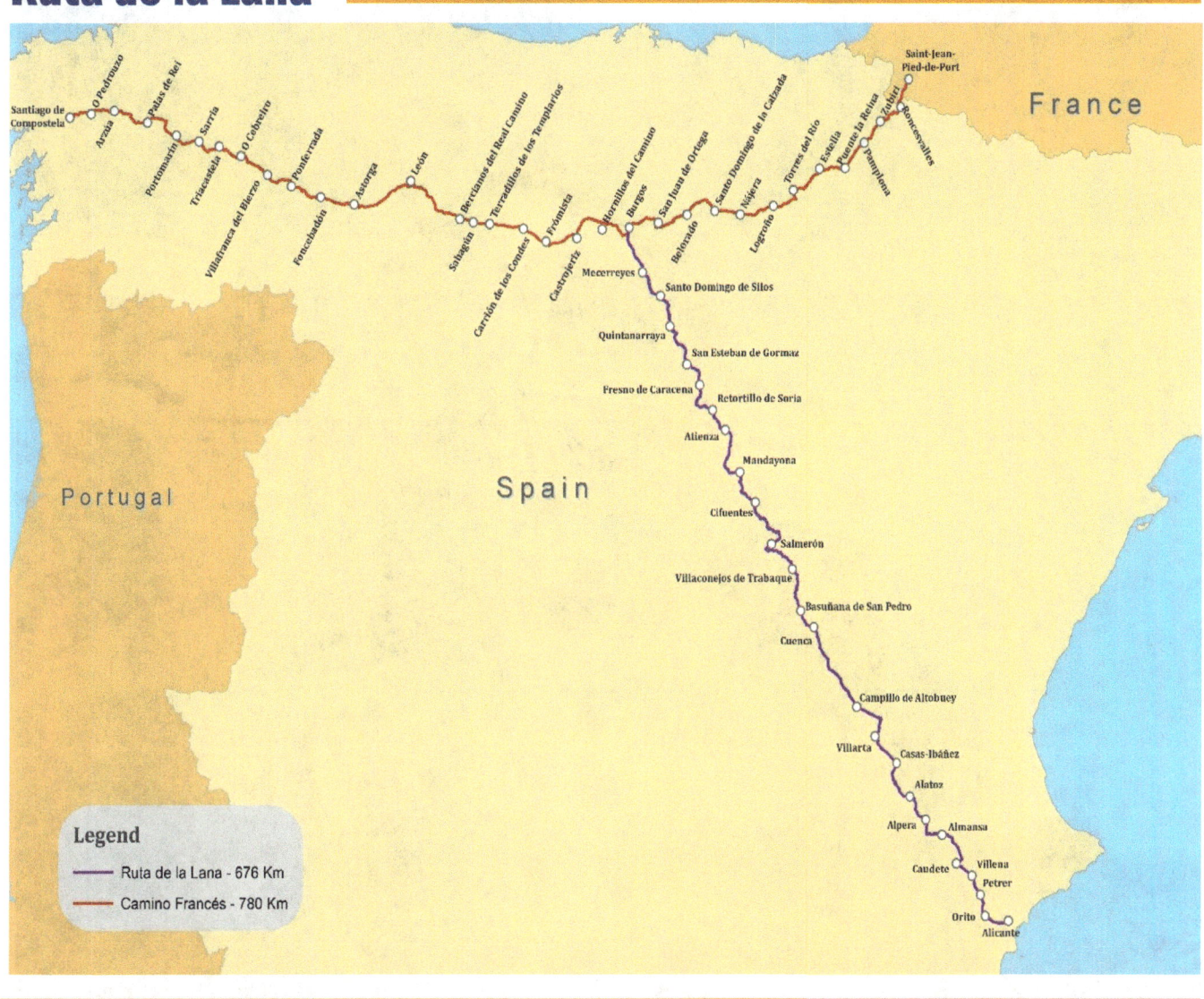

676 kilometers (410 miles)　　25 to 30 days　　Difficult

The Ruta de la Lana ("Wool Route") is one of the longer and more demanding alternative Caminos, stretching approximately 676 kilometers (410 miles) from Alicante to Burgos, where it connects with the Camino Francés for the final stretch to Santiago de Compostela. Pilgrims typically take 25 to 30 days to complete this path, encountering a mix of flat plains and rolling hills along the way.

Unlike the more frequently traveled routes, the Ruta de la Lana follows the same ancient paths once used by merchants and shepherds transporting wool from the fertile lands of Castile to the Mediterranean coast. This historical significance is reflected in the architecture, traditions, and warm hospitality of the towns along the way, offering an experience that blends cultural discovery with the spiritual essence of the Camino.

One of the most notable stops is the city of Cuenca, renowned for its "Casas Colgadas" (Hanging Houses), a striking example of medieval engineering, with timber balconies suspended dramatically over a cliffside. This UNESCO-listed town is a cultural gem, where history and artistry converge in its well-preserved old quarter.

Further along the route, Villanueva de la Jara presents a quintessential Spanish village experience, where locals welcome pilgrims with open arms. Here, travelers can engage with age-old traditions, explore historic churches, and savor local cuisine, reinforcing the Camino's enduring theme of community and connection.

The Ruta de la Lana takes pilgrims through a rich tapestry of landscapes, from the semi-arid plains of Alicante to the rolling hills and woodlands of Castilla-La Mancha, eventually merging with the green pastures of northern Spain. The route is physically demanding, with long distances between towns and fewer pilgrim facilities compared to more popular routes. However, for those seeking solitude, adventure, and a deep sense of pilgrimage, this Camino offers a unique and rewarding journey.

This route is ideal for experienced walkers or those looking for a longer, more immersive pilgrimage, offering a truly authentic experience away from the crowds. The combination of historical significance, breathtaking landscapes, and strong local traditions makes it a remarkable choice for those who want to connect deeply with Spain's past while embracing the spiritual essence of the Camino.

Camino de Invierno

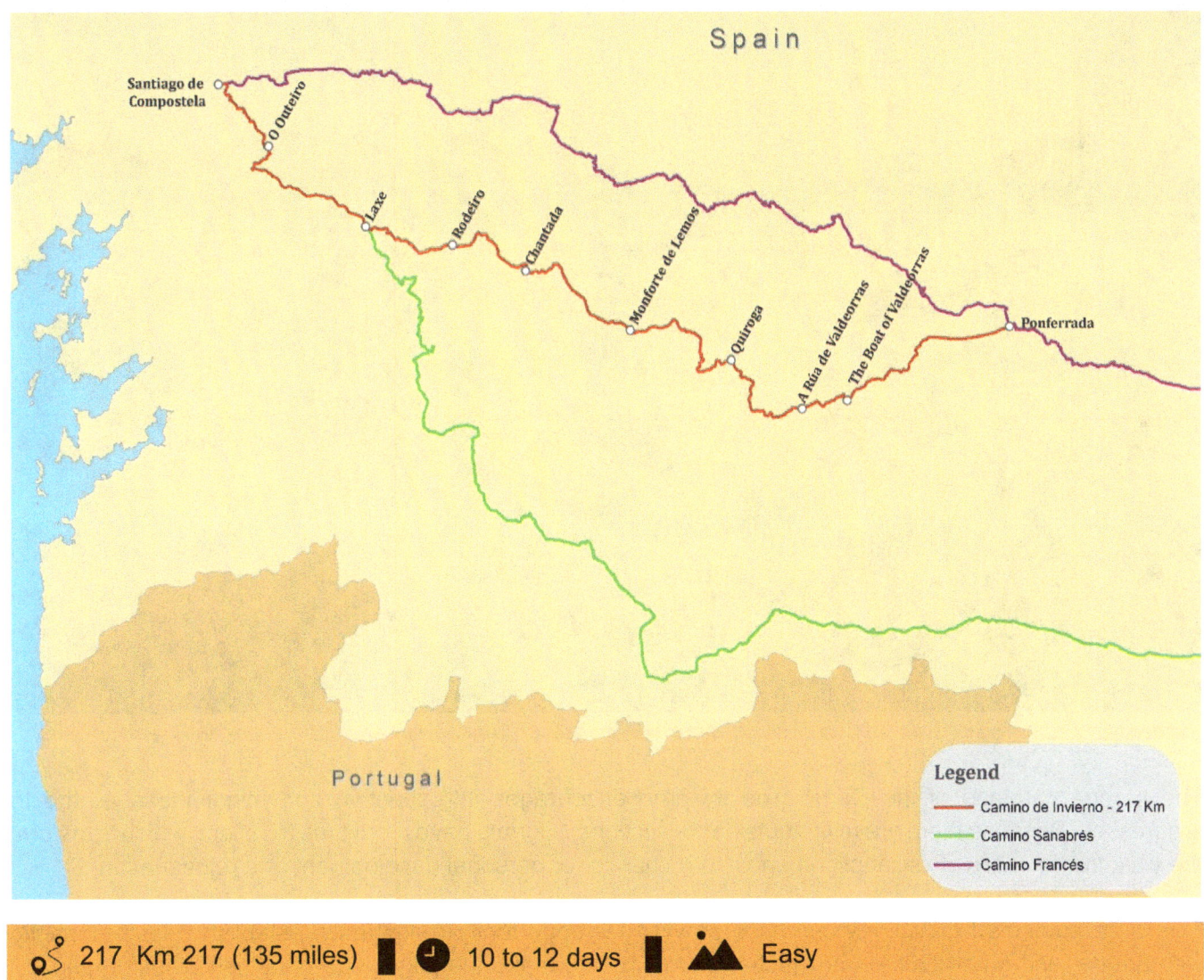

🧭 217 Km 217 (135 miles) ⏱ 10 to 12 days ⛰ Easy

The Camino de Invierno, or Winter Way, is a quieter, lesser-traveled alternative that offers a more intimate pilgrimage experience. Covering 217 kilometers (135 miles), it takes approximately 10 to 12 days, allowing for a relaxed pace to fully absorb the journey without the crowds found on more popular routes.

Winding through Galicia's picturesque landscapes, the path reveals rolling hills, lush valleys, and peaceful countryside. The terrain is varied but manageable, making it an attractive option for both experienced walkers and those new to long-distance hiking. Unlike the steeper climbs of other Camino routes, this path offers a gentler ascent, allowing pilgrims to focus on the beauty of the surroundings rather than physical strain.

Among its most notable stops is Monforte de Lemos, a historic town where medieval architecture, a majestic castle, and welcoming taverns bring Galicia's rich heritage to life. Here, traditional cuisine made from locally sourced ingredients invites travelers to savor the region's flavors. Further along, the town of A Rúa offers another rewarding pause, where vineyards producing renowned Galician wines line the route, offering a taste of the region's deep-rooted winemaking traditions.

The serene cadence of the Camino de Invierno encourages introspection and mindfulness as the trip progresses. Because there are fewer outside distractions, pilgrims have more time to reflect, which transforms the walk from a mere physical pilgrimage into a chance for personal development and rejuvenation.

This route redefines the Camino experience, providing an opportunity to slow down, establish a close connection with nature, and embrace the unexpected moments that make the pilgrimage genuinely transforming. It is more than just a more sedate option.

CHAPTER 7: CAMINO PORTUGUÉS

CENTRAL VS. COASTAL ROUTES COMPARISON

The Camino Portugués offers pilgrims two distinct paths to Santiago de Compostela, each with its own unique set of experiences, landscapes, and challenges. The Central Route, more traditionally trodden, carves through the heart of Portugal and into Spain, providing a blend of cultural immersion and historical exploration. In contrast, the Coastal Route, with its scenic vistas along the Atlantic Ocean, presents a different appeal, combining the rugged beauty of the coastline with quieter, less crowded paths.

The Central Route begins in Lisbon, Portugal's vibrant capital, and stretches approximately 616 kilometers to Santiago de Compostela. This path takes pilgrims through a variety of landscapes, from urban centers and agricultural fields to dense forests and serene riversides. The trek from Lisbon to Porto is known for its solitude and sparse pilgrim infrastructure, testing both physical endurance and mental fortitude. However, the road gets more crowded after Porto, where pilgrims can meet others and find a variety of amenities to meet their needs. Coimbra and Tui, two important cities along this route, have rich historical narratives and architectural wonders, ranging from Gothic churches to old Roman ruins, offering a comprehensive look into the peninsula's past. Pilgrims can also explore local traditions, such as the famous Fado music in Lisbon and the vibrant markets in Coimbra, enhancing their cultural experience.

In contrast, the Coastal Route, starting from Porto, runs along the Atlantic coast before turning inland towards Santiago. This path is approximately 265 kilometers long, significantly shorter than its Central counterpart, and is characterized by its maritime landscapes. Pilgrims walking this route enjoy the refreshing ocean breeze, stunning beaches, and picturesque fishing villages. The terrain here is generally flat, and while physically less demanding, the exposure to the elements—sun, wind, and rain—can present its own set of challenges. The Coastal Route also offers a unique cultural experience, with opportunities to indulge in the region's seafood cuisine and to explore its Celtic influences, which are particularly evident in the Galician segment of the route. The vibrant coastal towns, such as Baiona and Combarro, provide a glimpse into the local way of life, with their bustling markets and traditional festivals.

In terms of difficulty, the Central Route is more physically demanding due to the longer distances between towns and the wider range of terrain. Pilgrims must prepare for days of extensive walking, often without the immediate comfort of nearby services. While easier in terms of physical effort due to its flatter terrain and shorter overall distance, the Coastal Route requires preparation for weather-related challenges, as coastal weather can be unpredictable. Pilgrims should be ready for sudden weather changes, packing layers and waterproof gear to ensure comfort throughout their journey.

The experience of walking these routes also differs significantly. The Central Route offers a more traditional Camino experience, fostering a stronger sense of community among pilgrims and more frequent encounters with historical and religious landmarks. It provides a deeper immersion into the Portuguese and Spanish cultures, with more opportunities to interact with locals and to participate in regional traditions. The Coastal Route appeals to those seeking solitude, reflection, and a connection with nature. It offers a quieter path, less crowded trails, and more personal space for spiritual contemplation, allowing pilgrims to connect deeply with their surroundings and themselves.

Depending on the pilgrim's choices, level of physical fitness, and intended experiences, they can choose between the Central and Coastal Routes of the Camino Portugués. The Central Route might be more satisfying for those seeking a conventional pilgrimage with plenty of cultural and historical experiences, while the Coastal Route might be more appealing to those seeking a more sedate, outdoor experience. Both routes provide pilgrims with life-changing experiences, leading them not only to Santiago de Compostela but also to a better comprehension of both the outside world and themselves.

Cultural Treasures and Scenic Highlights

The Camino Portugués' scenic attractions and cultural treasures, which include both the Central and Coastal Routes, provide a wide range of experiences that satisfy pilgrims' desires for spiritual enrichment, beauty, and history. The walk's physical difficulty is compellingly complemented by the sights and historical and cultural value of the places along the route in Portugal and Spain.

Discovering the historic city of Coimbra, a UNESCO World Heritage site, is a must-do while traveling the Central Route. This city offers pilgrims a tranquil respite from the strenuousness of the journey by allowing them to stroll through its historic academic halls and verdant botanical gardens, which are home to one of the oldest continuously operating universities in the world. The Roman remains of Conímbriga, a short diversion from Coimbra, provide an intriguing look into Portugal's ancient past with their well-preserved mosaics and architectural fragments that highlight the region's historical strata.

Figure 7. Coimbra

As the Central Route crosses into Spain, the fortress town of Valença do Minho stands out with its impressive walls and breathtaking views over the Minho River. The transition from Portugal into Spain via the Tui International Bridge symbolizes a significant milestone in the pilgrimage, highlighting the transformative power of such experiences.

Figure 8. Minho River

The Coastal Route presents a different array of experiences with its stunning maritime landscapes. The seaside town of Viana do Castelo, featuring the majestic Sanctuary of Santa Luzia atop a hill, offers unforgettable panoramic views of the Atlantic Ocean. The town, rich in maritime history, beautiful plazas, and baroque architecture, encourages leisurely exploration and cultural immersion, allowing for a genuine connection with the surroundings

Figure 9. Sanctuary of Santa Luzia

Further along the Coastal Route, the fishing village of A Guarda showcases a unique cultural highlight with Monte Santa Trega. This Celtic settlement, dating back to 2000 BC, provides an intriguing look into the pre-Roman inhabitants of the region. The archaeological site and museum display artifacts and structures that offer valuable insights into the lives of these ancient people, while the hilltop location rewards visitors with sweeping views of the ocean and surrounding landscapes.

Figure 10. Monte de Santa Trega

The Galician village of Padrón, where the remains of Saint James are thought to have landed, is where the two pathways converge. Many pilgrims find inspiration and introspection at the town's botanical park, which is home to the fabled Santiaguiño do Monte, where Saint James is supposed to have preached. Additionally, Padrón is known for its peppers, and indulging in this regional specialty can improve the pilgrimage experience.

The Camino Portugués, whether along the Central or Coastal Route, features cultural treasures and scenic highlights that enrich the experience. Ancient ruins, historic cities, breathtaking landscapes, and quaint fishing villages deepen the understanding of the regions traversed, adding layers of meaning to the pilgrim's experience. Engaging with these landmarks and the surrounding communities creates a unique opportunity to connect with local culture, history, and spirituality, transforming the physical act of walking into a path of discovery and personal growth.

Practical Tips for a Smooth Journey

Preparing for the Camino Portugués requires careful planning to ensure a smooth and fulfilling experience. Here are practical tips covering **accommodation, border crossings, best travel seasons,** and strategies to **avoid common pitfalls.**

Accommodation: It is strongly advised to make reservations in advance, particularly during the busiest times of the year (April to October). It's advisable to book lodging in important cities like Coimbra, Porto, and Tui on the Central Route at least a few weeks before your arrival. The Coastal Route, while generally less crowded, experiences an influx of travelers in seaside towns during the summer months. Use pilgrim-specific platforms and apps for reservations and always maintain a list of backup options in case your first choice is unavailable. Many albergues do not accept reservations and operate on a first-come, first-served basis, so arriving early in the day can significantly increase your chances of securing a spot.

Border Crossings: The transition from Portugal to Spain is straightforward, with the Tui International Bridge serving as the main crossing point for pilgrims on the Central Route. Keep your travel documents up to date and easily accessible. While border checks are rare within the Schengen Area, having proper identification is essential for checking into accommodations and in case of emergencies.

Best Travel Seasons: The ideal months to walk the Camino Portugués are May, June, September, and early October. These periods offer milder weather, fewer crowds, and a more comfortable walking experience. July and August are the busiest and hottest months, which can lead to overcrowded trails and accommodations. For those walking the Coastal Route, early fall is particularly appealing as the summer heat subsides, yet the ocean remains warm enough for swimming.

Avoiding Common Pitfalls:

- Overpacking: Carry only what you need. A common mistake is bringing too much, which can lead to physical strain and discomfort. Aim for a backpack weight that is no more than 10% of your body weight. Essentials include lightweight clothing layers, a good quality rain jacket, a sun hat, sunscreen, a basic first aid kit, and reliable walking shoes.

- Underestimating the Terrain: While the Coastal Route is known for its flat paths, the Central Route can be challenging with its varied terrain. Incorporate hill training and long-distance walks into your preparation to build endurance and strength, setting yourself up for success.

- Neglecting Foot Care: Blisters and foot pain are among the top reasons pilgrims struggle on the Camino. Invest in well-fitting, broken-in footwear and moisture-wicking socks. Practice good foot hygiene by drying your feet thoroughly and changing socks mid-day to prevent blisters.

- Ignoring the Weather: The weather on the Camino Portugués can be unpredictable, with sudden rain showers and temperature changes. Always check the forecast and prepare with appropriate clothing and gear, ensuring you're ready for anything.

- Skip travel Insurance: Obtain travel insurance that covers medical emergencies, trip cancellations, and lost baggage. This is crucial for peace of mind and protection against unforeseen circumstances.

Pilgrims can navigate the Camino Portugués with confidence by following these practical tips and focusing on the spiritual, cultural, and personal growth aspects of their experience. The Camino serves as a test of physical endurance and an opportunity for reflection and connection. With proper preparation and mindfulness, you can face the challenges and rewards that this ancient path offers.

Camino Espiritual

The Camino Espiritual, or Spiritual Way, is a lesser-known yet profoundly enriching variant of the Camino Portugués, designed for those seeking a deeper, more contemplative pilgrimage. Unlike the more traveled paths leading to Santiago, this route encourages a slower, introspective experience, allowing pilgrims to engage with their surroundings, history, and personal reflections on a much deeper level.

This route diverges from the traditional Camino Portugués, guiding travelers through serene landscapes, ancient monasteries, and peaceful rural settings that foster mindfulness and meditation. It typically begins in Tui, where pilgrims cross the Tui International Bridge into Spain, marking the start of a pilgrimage that prioritizes inner exploration over physical endurance.

As pilgrims move along this path, they pass through quaint villages, medieval churches, and tranquil forests, each offering a space for reflection and solitude. The less crowded nature of this route allows for a more personal connection with the environment, creating an atmosphere where pilgrims can walk in silence, appreciate the natural beauty around them, and engage in meaningful conversations with fellow travelers. Many choose this path as a retreat from the distractions of daily life, embracing the simplicity of walking as a way to reconnect with themselves and their spiritual beliefs.

Beyond its tranquil atmosphere, the Camino Espiritual is steeped in history and sacred traditions. One of the most significant sites along the route is the Monastery of San Juan de Padrón, a place deeply linked to the legend of Saint James. According to tradition, the boat carrying the remains of the apostle docked here when it arrived in Galicia. Pilgrims who walk this path often feel a strong sense of reverence as they pass through locations tied to the origins of the Santiago pilgrimage.

Additionally, the Ruta da Pedra e da Auga (Path of Stone and Water) is a breathtaking section of the route, leading pilgrims along a scenic trail of old water mills, rivers, and dense woodlands. This segment embodies the essence of the Spiritual Camino, where nature and history merge to create an atmosphere of peace, renewal, and quiet reflection.

One of the most unique aspects of this pilgrimage is the Traslatio, a symbolic boat journey across the Ulla River, replicating the legendary final voyage of Saint James' remains. This experience adds a profound spiritual dimension to the pilgrimage, allowing pilgrims to reflect on the journey's purpose and meaning as they sail toward Padrón, a town historically considered the gateway to Santiago.

CHAPTER 8: CAMINO PRIMITIVO

• • • • •

CHALLENGES AND REWARDS ON THE OLDEST ROUTE

The Original Way, often called the Camino Primitivo, is a historic route that follows the paths of the first pilgrims to Santiago de Compostela. This route begins in Oviedo and stretches approximately 321 kilometers (200 miles) to Santiago, offering a passage through the rugged landscapes of Asturias and Galicia. Its demanding nature, characterized by steep ascents, remote mountain paths and unpredictable weather, poses challenges even for the most seasoned hikers. Yet, this very rigor attracts adventurous pilgrims eager to engage in not just a physical test but also a profound spiritual and personal exploration.

Historical Significance: The Camino Primitivo holds a special place in the history of the Camino de Santiago. It is believed to be the path taken by King Alfonso II the Chaste in the 9th century from the Asturian capital of Oviedo to the newly discovered tomb of Saint James in Santiago. This historical context adds a rich layer of meaning to the experience as pilgrims walk a path that has served as a spiritual conduit for more than a millennium.

Terrain and Scenery: The route traverses some of the most breathtaking landscapes in northern Spain. From the verdant valleys of Asturias to the rugged mountains of the Cantabrian Range, pilgrims enjoy stunning vistas that are unparalleled on other Camino routes. The passage through the Hospitales Route, one of the most challenging yet visually rewarding sections, provides panoramic views of the Asturian wilderness, showcasing the untamed beauty of Spain's northern frontier.

Spiritual Rewards: The solitude and natural beauty of the Camino Primitivo create a unique setting for introspection and spiritual renewal. The physical challenges of the route, combined with the quieter trails, encourage pilgrims to explore their motivations and experiences. This reflective experience can lead to profound personal insights and a renewed sense of purpose.

Cultural Encounters: Despite its remote paths, the Camino Primitivo passes through ancient towns and villages where the traditional way of life remains preserved. Pilgrims can engage with local customs and traditions, enjoy the hospitality of small communities, and experience the rich cultural heritage of the region. Sampling hearty Asturian cuisine and exploring medieval churches and sanctuaries allows for a deep dive into the cultural mosaic of northern Spain.

Preparation and Logistics: Given its demanding nature, thorough preparation is essential for those undertaking the Camino Primitivo. Physical training builds stamina and strength, particularly for the mountainous sections, while careful planning of stages ensures accommodation in remote areas. Pilgrims should prepare for sudden weather changes and carry appropriate gear for both warm and cold conditions. Despite these challenges, the infrastructure along the route, including well-marked trails and pilgrim hostels (albergues), enables travelers to navigate the path with confidence.

Community and Camaraderie: The Camino Primitivo fosters a strong sense of community among pilgrims. Shared challenges and experiences along the route create bonds that often last a lifetime. The smaller number of travelers, compared to more popular routes like the Camino Francés, allows faces to become familiar and friendships to form quickly. This camaraderie plays a key role in the Camino experience, providing support and encouragement through the most challenging sections of the path.

Wild Terrain and Remote Beauty

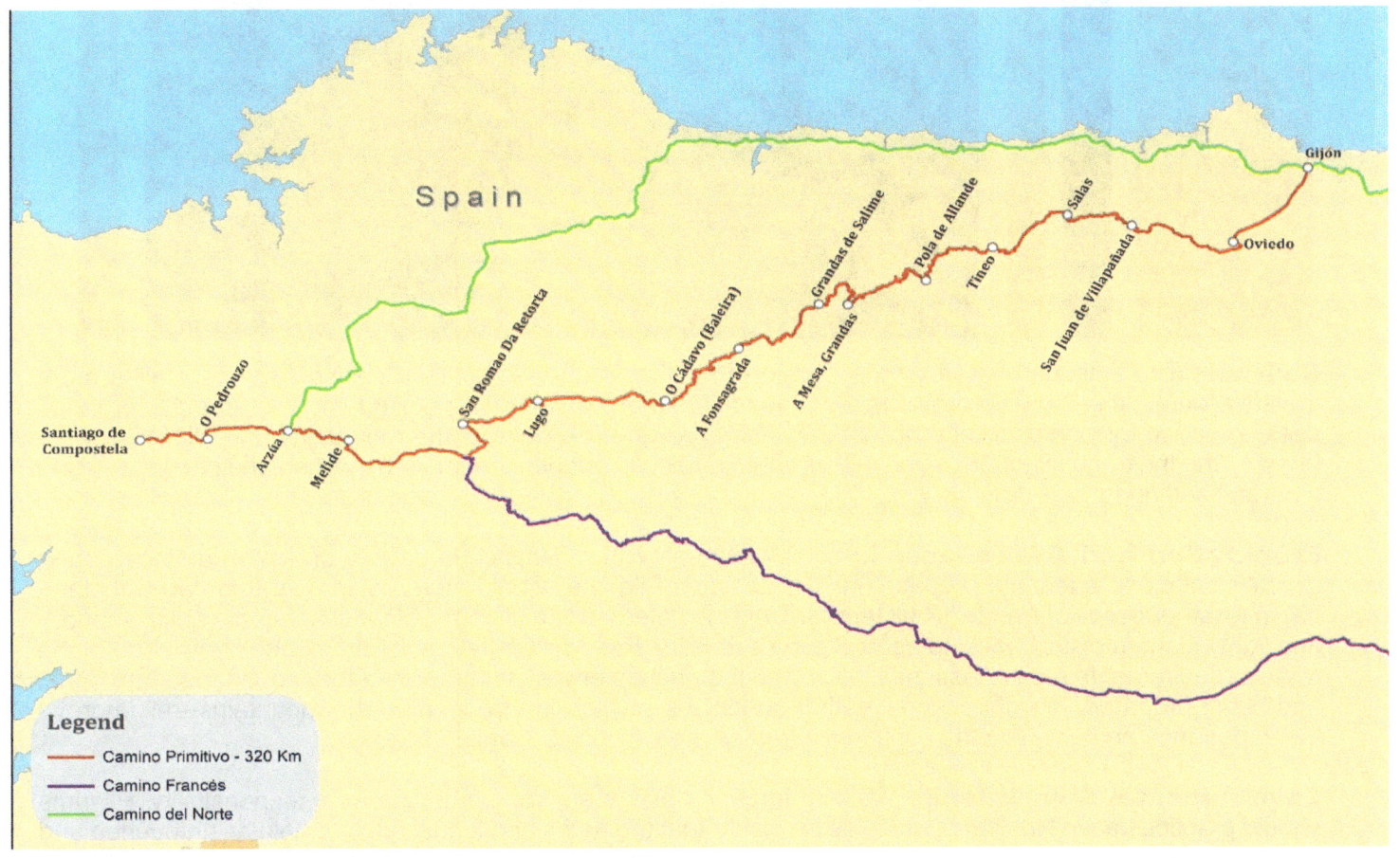

The Camino Primitivo unfolds through some of Spain's most untouched and wild terrains, offering pilgrims a path through landscapes that challenge and inspire. Rough terrain, including steep mountain trails, thick forests, and tranquil river basins, contribute to the route's secluded attractiveness. These natural features provide a setting for a pilgrimage that emphasizes both introspection and exploration of the outside world.

Rugged Landscapes: The diverse terrain of the Camino Primitivo presents a variety of challenges. Pilgrims navigate the steep ascents and descents of the Cantabrian Mountains, where rocky paths demand careful footing and a steady pace. These sections test physical endurance and mental resolve. However, the rewards include unparalleled views of Asturias and Galicia's wild countryside, with sweeping vistas that extend for miles on clear days, showcasing the beauty that awaits those who persevere.

Mountain Paths: The mountain paths of the Camino Primitivo define the experience. These trails wind through ancient forests, past remote hillside villages, and across high mountain passes. The 'Hospitales' Route stands out as a highlight for many pilgrims. Named for the medieval hospitals that once served travelers along this path, it offers some of the Camino's most dramatic scenery. Walking these paths often places one above the cloud line, immersed in a landscape that feels both timeless and untouched, fostering a deep connection with nature.

Solitude: The solitude offered by the Camino Primitivo is one of its most striking aspects. Unlike more traveled routes, the Primitivo provides a profound sense of isolation. This solitude serves as a gift for those seeking space for personal reflection and spiritual growth. The quiet of the mountains, the stillness of the forests, and the tranquility of the river valleys contribute to an atmosphere of introspection and peace, creating a perfect setting for self-discovery.

Preparation and Awareness: To completely enjoy the Camino Primitivo's untamed landscape and isolated splendor, adequate preparation is necessary. Pilgrims should have equipment that can withstand harsh weather conditions and difficult terrain. Trekking poles, strong hiking boots with adequate ankle support, and lightweight, moisture-wicking apparel are necessary. Respect for the environment and knowledge of the route's requirements are still essential. Knowing the phases of the trip, preparing for enough food and drink, and being prepared for unforeseen weather conditions—which are frequent in the mountains—all improve the experience and give you the confidence to face the difficulties that lie ahead.

Environmental Stewardship: Walking through pristine environments carries a responsibility. Pilgrims should practice Leave No Trace principles to ensure that the paths and landscapes remain as untouched and beautiful for future travelers as they are today. This includes packing out all trash, staying on marked trails to prevent erosion, and being mindful of wildlife. Each traveler contributes to preserving the natural beauty that makes this experience so special.

The wild terrain and remote beauty of the Camino Primitivo create a unique pilgrimage experience. This route challenges and rewards in equal measure, fostering deep connections to nature, history, and oneself. For thoughtful and adventurous travelers, it transforms the spirit and leaves an indelible mark on the heart.

What to Expect Along the Way

Navigating the Camino Primitivo requires knowledge of its daily stages, key towns, and available accommodation options, along with essential preparation tips to ensure a fulfilling experience. This section explores these aspects, providing a roadmap for what pilgrims can expect while traversing this ancient path.

Daily Stages: The Camino Primitivo divides into manageable daily stages, typically ranging from 15 to 25 kilometers (9 to 15 miles), depending on the terrain and the pilgrim's physical condition. Starting from Oviedo, the route passes through various landscapes, including steep mountain passes and lush valleys. Key stages include the ascent to the Hospitales Route, the descent into Lugo, and the final stretch toward Santiago de Compostela. Each stage presents its challenges and rewards, with longer distances requiring robust physical preparation and shorter stages allowing more time to explore and reflect on the path ahead.

Key Towns: Pilgrims encounter towns rich in history and culture along the way. Grado, Salas, and Tineo showcase Asturian heritage, featuring well-preserved medieval architecture and local markets. Pola de Allande and Berducedo offer essential services and a glimpse into rural life. The ancient Roman walls of Lugo serve as a cultural landmark, providing pilgrims a chance to rest and explore. Each town possesses its unique charm, creating opportunities for cultural immersion and meaningful interactions with locals.

Figure 12. The ancient Roman walls of Lugo

Accommodation Options: The Camino Primitivo, while less crowded than other routes, offers a variety of accommodations, from traditional albergues (pilgrim hostels) to private guesthouses and hotels. Albergues represent the most budget-friendly option, providing communal sleeping areas and basic amenities. Booking in advance proves advisable, especially in smaller towns with limited options. Some stages require careful planning to secure accommodation, particularly during peak pilgrimage seasons. Pilgrims should evaluate their comfort levels and budget when selecting accommodations, balancing the desire for solitude with the camaraderie found in communal lodgings.

Essential Preparation Tips:

- Physical Training: Start a training regimen several months in advance to prepare for the route's challenging terrain. Focus on building endurance through long walks, incorporating varied terrain to simulate the conditions of the Camino.

- Gear Selection: Invest in high-quality, lightweight gear. A durable pair of hiking boots, a comfortable backpack with a rain cover, and moisture-wicking clothing are essential. Consider the season of your pilgrimage when selecting gear, as weather conditions can vary.

- Navigation Skills: Although the Camino Primitivo is well-marked, carrying a detailed map or a GPS device provides additional security. Familiarize yourself with the route's stages and key landmarks to enhance your navigation confidence.

- Language Basics: Learning basic Spanish phrases enriches your experience, allowing smoother interactions with locals and fellow pilgrims.

- Mental Preparation: The Camino offers opportunities for personal growth and spiritual exploration. Prepare for the solitude and reflection that the Camino Primitivo presents, embracing the chance for self-discovery.

CHAPTER 9: CAMINO DEL NORTE

COASTAL BEAUTY AND RUGGED TRAILS

Offering pilgrims breathtaking vistas of the Atlantic Ocean, the Camino del Norte fascinates with its coastal panoramas that run along Spain's northern shore. This route offers a combination of natural beauty and cultural diversity with its rough routes winding through the Basque Country, Cantabria, Asturias, and Galicia.

As you traverse Spain's varied ecosystems and historical legacy, walking the Camino del Norte challenges your physical stamina and encourages you to enjoy each minute.

Coastal Landscapes: The Camino del Norte provides an unparalleled experience of walking alongside the ocean, with numerous opportunities to witness the powerful beauty of the Atlantic. A haven for nature enthusiasts, the route features breathtaking cliffs, remote beaches, and estuaries brimming with wildlife. The sound of waves crashing against the shore accompanies pilgrims, creating a soothing backdrop for the experience. Key coastal towns along the way, such as San Sebastián, Santander, and Gijón, offer stunning ocean views and a chance to indulge in the local maritime culture, enhancing your experience with memorable moments.

Rugged Trails: The terrain of the Camino del Norte varies and presents challenges, with paths that climb steep hills, descend into lush valleys, and navigate rocky coastlines. These trails require a good level of fitness and preparation, as they can be physically demanding. However, the effort rewards you with secluded paths, away from the crowds of more popular routes, and intimate encounters with the natural landscape. Appreciate the diversity of the terrain, allowing yourself to experience the changing landscapes of northern Spain, from the green hills of the Basque Country to the rugged cliffs of Asturias.

Unique Appeal: The Camino del Norte stands out due to its combination of natural beauty, cultural encounters, and historical sites. This route passes through regions known for their distinct identities, languages, and culinary traditions. Pilgrims can taste regional specialties, such as Basque pintxos, Cantabrian seafood, and Asturian cider, enriching their experience with gastronomic delights. The route also provides opportunities to visit significant historical landmarks, including Gothic cathedrals, ancient monasteries, and prehistoric caves, offering a deeper understanding of Spain's rich cultural tapestry.

Preparation Tips:

- **Physical Readiness:** Preparing physically for the Camino del Norte is crucial due to the challenging terrain. Incorporate hill training and long-distance walks into your routine to build stamina and strength, empowering you to tackle the trails with confidence.

- **Gear Selection:** Choose footwear that provides support and grip for rocky and uneven paths. A lightweight, waterproof backpack is essential to carry your belongings while protecting them from rain. A windbreaker or rain jacket will shield you against unpredictable coastal weather, ensuring you're ready for anything Mother Nature throws your way.

- **Navigation Skills:** Although the route is marked with traditional yellow arrows and scallop shells, carrying a detailed guidebook or a GPS device enhances navigation through less populated areas and helps you stay on the correct path, giving you peace of mind as you progress.

- **Cultural Engagement:** Take time to learn about the regions you will pass through. Familiarizing yourself with local customs, basic language skills, and historical context will enrich your experience and foster meaningful interactions with locals and fellow pilgrims, transforming your walk into a cultural exploration.

The Camino del Norte presents physical challenges alongside spiritual and cultural enrichment. The stunning coastal landscapes, combined with the rugged trails, create a memorable experience through some of Spain's most captivating scenery. With adequate preparation and an open heart, pilgrims on the Camino del Norte will discover the transformative power of walking through these diverse and beautiful landscapes.

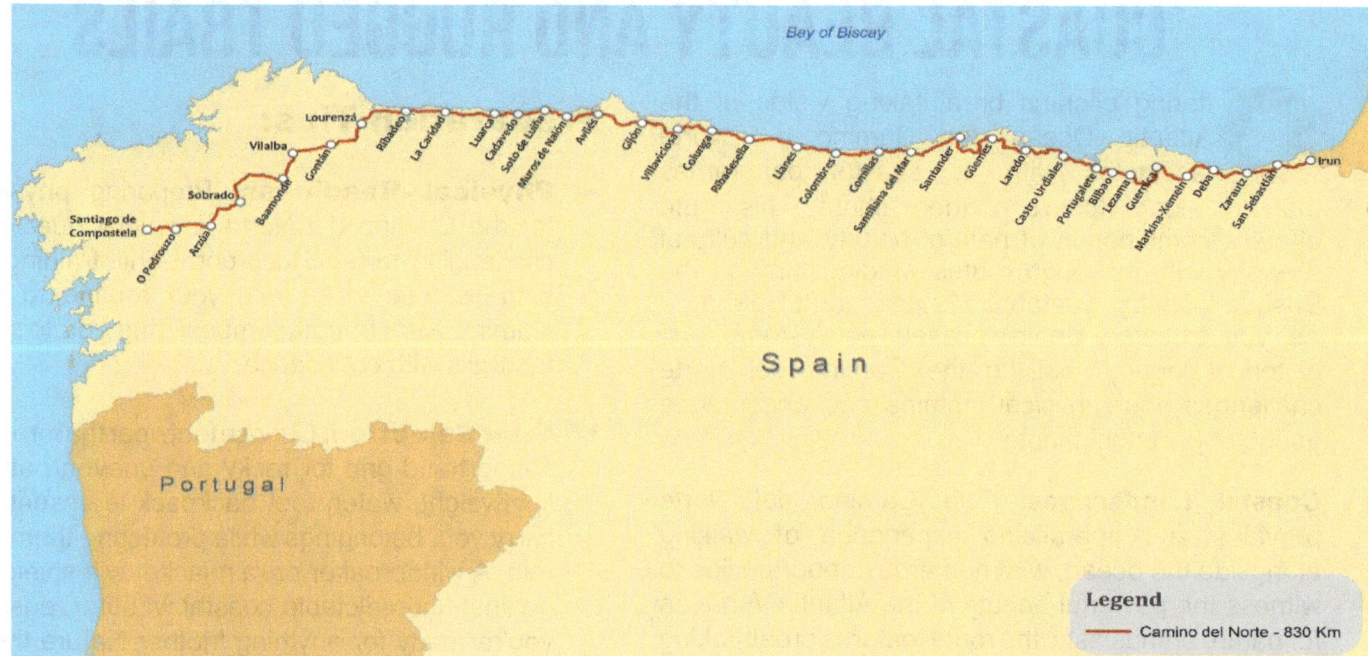

Scenic Detours and Hidden Beaches

Leaving the Camino del Norte's main route offers pilgrims a wealth of picturesque detours and undiscovered beaches that promise tranquility and stunning natural beauty, providing a special chance to get closer to the environment. By leading to remote locations where the virgin sand and the rhythm of the waves provide the ideal setting for introspection and renewal, these less-traveled routes encourage a spirit of exploration and adventure.

One such detour is the path to Playa del Silencio, a stunning beach nestled between cliffs, where the sound of the ocean fills the air, undisturbed by the hustle and bustle of tourist spots. The beach is accessible via a short hike from the main trail, providing a peaceful retreat for those looking to immerse themselves in nature's tranquility. The clear waters and unique rock formations make it an ideal spot for contemplation and photography, capturing the essence of the Camino's natural wonders.

Figure 14. Playa del Silencio

Another hidden gem is the coastal path near Cudillero, a picturesque fishing village that boasts vibrant houses perched on the cliffs and a labyrinth of narrow streets. A detour through this village offers a glimpse into the local maritime culture and leads to small, secluded beaches that are perfect for a quiet afternoon rest. The charm of Cudillero, combined with the serene beauty of its surrounding beaches, creates a memorable experience that beautifully contrasts the more rugged aspects of the Camino del Norte.

For those willing to explore further off the beaten path, the route to Cabo de Peñas presents an opportunity to discover the northernmost point of Asturias. This detour takes pilgrims through a landscape characterized by dramatic cliffs and expansive sea views, culminating at a lighthouse that stands as a sentinel over the rugged coastline. The area around Cabo de Peñas is known for its rich birdlife and diverse flora, making it a haven for nature enthusiasts and a peaceful escape for those seeking solitude.

Figure 15. Cabo de Peñas

Planning these scenic detours and hidden beaches into the Camino requires careful consideration and an openness to explore beyond the traditional route. Pilgrims should account for the extra time and effort these detours may require, ensuring they have adequate supplies and are prepared for varying terrain. However, discovering these off-route gems offers immeasurable rewards, providing moments of solitude, beauty, and a deeper connection with the natural world surrounding the Camino del Norte.

Uncovering these hidden spots along the Camino del Norte enriches the pilgrimage, providing a unique perspective on the landscape and culture of northern Spain. Whether experiencing quiet reflection at a secluded beach, enjoying the charm of a coastal village, or taking in the awe-inspiring views from a rugged cliff, these scenic detours offer a profound sense of discovery and fulfillment that complements the spiritual experience of the Camino. Pilgrims who choose the path less traveled find themselves rewarded with moments of beauty and tranquility that resonate long after their time on the Camino de Santiago.

Best Places to Eat, Stay, and Explore

For those planning to experience the Camino del Norte, finding the right places to eat, stay, and explore is crucial for a fulfilling experience. This section provides detailed recommendations to help make your pilgrimage enriching and comfortable.

Accommodations along the Camino del Norte range from traditional albergues to luxurious hotels, catering to various preferences and budgets. In San Sebastián, consider the **Hostel a Room in the City,** which offers both private and shared rooms, creating a comfortable and social atmosphere for pilgrims. For a more secluded experience, **Casa Rural Arboliz** in Ibarrangelu provides stunning sea views and a peaceful setting, ideal for rejuvenating your spirit. In the heart of Asturias, the **Hotel Rural Suquin** in Navia serves as a great stop to rest, featuring comfortable rooms and excellent service to help you recharge.

Dining on the Camino del Norte presents a delightful exploration of the diverse culinary landscape of northern Spain. In Bilbao, try **pintxos** at **Gure Toki**, which is known for its innovative take on this Basque specialty. Seafood lovers will enjoy the offerings at **Casa Salvador** in Cudillero, where the freshest catch is served daily, ensuring a memorable meal. For a taste of Asturian cider and traditional dishes, **Sidrería Casa Niembro** in Asiego provides a quintessential local dining experience, complete with breathtaking views of the Picos de Europa.

Exploration plays a vital role in the Camino del Norte, with numerous cultural and natural sites to discover. The **Guggenheim Museum** in Bilbao stands out for its stunning architecture and contemporary art collections that inspire creativity. The **Altamira Cave,** near Santillana del Mar, offers a fascinating glimpse into prehistoric art, though visits are limited to the replica cave to preserve the original paintings. For a spiritual experience, the **Monastery of Santo Toribio de Liébana** ranks among the oldest Christian monasteries in the world and serves as a pilgrimage site in its own right, housing the Lignum Crucis, the largest piece of the True Cross. When planning your stops along the Camino del Norte, keep these tips in mind:

- **Book in advance** during peak seasons to secure your preferred accommodations.
- **Explore local markets for fresh, regional produce to enjoy a picnic with a view.**
- **Engage with locals** to discover hidden gems and off-the-beaten-path experiences that can enrich your experience.

Careful selection of where to eat, stay, and explore enhances the Camino del Norte experience, blending physical challenge with cultural immersion and culinary delight. Each stop provides an opportunity to connect with the local community, savor regional flavors, and rest in comfort, preparing you for the next stage of your pilgrimage.

CHAPTER 10: CAMINO INGLÉS

THE PERFECT SHORT OPTION FOR BEGINNERS

Often recognized for covering a comparatively shorter distance than other Camino routes, the Camino Inglés is a great option for novices or those with limited time but still wanting to fully experience the Camino. The roughly 75-mile journey from Ferrol to Santiago de Compostela may be easily finished in a week, which makes it a desirable choice for pilgrims looking for a shorter yet profoundly enlightening experience.

Because of the time commitment and physical challenges, many people find the idea of going on a pilgrimage like the Camino de Santiago intimidating. By providing a moderate but genuine pilgrimage experience, the Camino Inglés minimizes these worries. The spiritual and cultural depth for which the Camino is renowned is not diminished by its shorter distance. Rather, it offers a concentrated dosage of the essence of the Camino, which makes it an ideal starting point for people who have never gone on a long-distance walking pilgrimage.

The route's historical significance adds to its appeal for beginners. Originating from the medieval period when English and Irish pilgrims landed in the ports of Ferrol or A Coruña, the Camino Inglés has a rich heritage that pilgrims can explore. This historical backdrop provides meaningful context to the experience, allowing pilgrims to connect with the past as they walk towards Santiago de Compostela.

Because the Camino Inglés has clearly marked and rather easy-to-follow routes, pilgrims may concentrate on the experience rather than worrying about getting lost. With enough signage, pilgrim hostels (albergues), and other facilities to meet the needs of walkers, the route's infrastructure is well-developed. This support structure and accessibility are essential for novices who might be worried about the pilgrimage's logistical details.

The physical demands of the Camino Inglés accommodate those who may not have extensive hiking experience. Although there are some mountainous sections, the terrain is generally less challenging than more arduous routes such as the Camino Primitivo or the Camino del Norte. This makes it an excellent choice for individuals seeking a pilgrimage that is physically manageable while still offering opportunities for personal reflection and challenge.

The Camino Inglés passes through a variety of landscapes, from coastal views to forested paths, providing a diverse and visually engaging experience. The route also allows pilgrims to experience the unique culture and cuisine of Galicia, from sampling the famous Galician octopus (pulpo a la gallega) to exploring the historic towns along the way. This cultural immersion is a key aspect of the Camino experience, offering insights into local traditions and a chance to connect with fellow pilgrims and locals alike.

The Camino Inglés is a useful but incredibly rewarding pilgrimage option for people with little time. It allows for a complete Camino experience, including obtaining the Compostela certificate upon reaching Santiago, within a condensed timeframe. This aspect appeals particularly to working professionals, retirees, or anyone with time constraints who wishes to partake in the transformative experience of the Camino de Santiago without committing to the longer routes.

The Camino Inglés stands out as the perfect short option for beginners or time-limited pilgrims due to its manageable distance, rich historical context, well-supported infrastructure, and the diverse cultural and natural landscapes it traverses. It provides a unique opportunity for spiritual exploration, serving as a gateway to the wider Camino experience and inspiring many to consider further pilgrimages in the future.

Solo Walking: Highlights and Safety Tips

Solo walkers on the Camino Inglés will discover a path filled with scenic beauty and spiritual solace, along with the camaraderie of fellow pilgrims. This shorter route offers breathtaking landscapes, historical sites, and opportunities for introspection and personal growth. Those venturing alone experience a unique blend of solitude and community, allowing for deep personal reflection while still benefiting from the safety of a well-trodden path.

Scenic Highlights for Solo Walkers:

Ferrol to Pontedeume: The initial stages of the Camino Inglés provide coastal views and the chance to walk through serene forests. Transitioning from urban to rural settings helps solo walkers adjust to the rhythm of the Camino, easing into the experience.

Figure 18. Fragas do Eume National Park

- Betanzos: A historical gem, Betanzos invites pilgrims to explore its medieval streets, Gothic churches, and the serene Betanzos River. Solo walkers can enjoy the tranquility of this town, taking time to reflect or journal while appreciating the peaceful atmosphere.

- Hospital de Bruma: Marking the midpoint of the Camino Inglés, this area is known for its rural landscapes and offers a peaceful setting for contemplation, fostering deeper insights and clarity.

- Sigueiro to Santiago de Compostela: The final stretch to Santiago brings anticipation and reflection. Approaching the city allows solo walkers to mentally prepare for the culmination of their experience, with the Cathedral of Santiago de Compostela serving as a powerful symbol of achievement and spiritual awakening.

Practical Advice for Solo Travelers:

- **Safety:** Always inform someone of your daily route and expected arrival time at your next destination. Carry a charged mobile phone with emergency numbers saved, including local police and accommodations. This simple step can provide peace of mind.

- **Packing:** Keep your pack light to avoid strain and injury. Essentials include a water bottle, snacks, a first-aid kit, sun protection, rain gear, and layers for changing weather. A whistle can be a useful tool for attracting attention in case of emergency, ensuring you're prepared for any situation.

- **Accommodations:** Book your stays in advance, especially during peak pilgrimage seasons. Many albergues offer communal dinners, which provide excellent opportunities for solo travelers to connect with others and share experiences.

- **Dining:** Solo walkers should explore local markets and cafes, where they can sample regional specialties. Dining alone can be a reflective experience, offering the chance to truly savor the local cuisine and culture, enhancing the overall experience.

- **Navigation:** Carry a detailed map and a guidebook. While the Camino Inglés is well-marked, having your own resources ensures you can always find your way. GPS apps on your smartphone can serve as a backup, keeping you on track.

Safety Considerations:

- **Stay on the Path:** The Camino Inglés is well-marked with yellow arrows and scallop shells. Straying from the path can lead to getting lost or inadvertently trespassing on private property, so sticking to the route ensures a smoother experience.

- **Trust Your Instincts**: If something doesn't feel right, trust your gut. Whether it's bypassing a sketchy shortcut or choosing to stay with a group, your intuition is a valuable tool on the Camino, guiding you safely along the way.

- **Health:** Listen to your body. Hydrate regularly, take breaks, and don't push beyond your limits. Solo walkers should be particularly mindful of their physical and mental health as they may not have immediate support from fellow pilgrims.

Connecting with Others:

While the experience is solo, the Camino fosters a sense of community. Engage with fellow pilgrims at rest stops, share stories, and offer support. Many solo walkers find that the Camino creates instant bonds through the shared goal of reaching Santiago de Compostela, enriching their experience.

The Camino Inglés for solo walkers serves as a path to self-discovery and personal growth. Adequate preparation, mindfulness of safety, and openness to experiences and people encountered along the way will lead solo pilgrims to a fulfilling and transformative Camino experience.

Cultural Stops Along the Way

The Camino Inglés presents pilgrims with a wealth of cultural treasures that enrich the experience beyond the physical walk. This route, steeped in history and tradition, offers a unique opportunity to explore the heart of Galician culture, revealing its rich tapestry of historical sites, charming towns, and enduring traditions. Each step along this path brings a deeper understanding of the essence of this ancient pilgrimage and the people who have shaped it over centuries.

One of the first significant cultural stops is the town of Ferrol, known for its naval history and as one of the traditional starting points for the Camino Inglés. The town's museums and architecture also reflect its history of naval architecture, giving travelers a window into the nautical legacy that has been so important to the growth of the area. By connecting with the innumerable pilgrims who have embarked on their journey from this ancient harbor, exploring Ferrol's alleys creates a feeling of continuity and connection.

The ancient bridge and the ruins of the Andrade Tower serve as reminders of the town's historical significance as the road meanders its way towards Pontedeume. With its curving, narrow paths and stone homes, Pontedeume's charming old town beckons pilgrims to stop and consider the years that have gone by and the many generations of visitors who have come through this entryway on their way to Santiago. Embracing the common experiences that unite us throughout ages is made possible by this moment.

The town of Betanzos, which lies further along, fascinates with its impressively maintained medieval architecture, which includes the Gothic cathedrals of Santa Maria and San Francisco. A highly spiritual event that creates a strong sense of connection with the local community and its traditions, Betanzos is well known for its Holy Week processions. For pilgrims wanting to experience Galician culture, the town's historic streets and squares, replete with the smells of regional cuisine, offer a warm relief and serve as a reminder of the delights of exploration and camaraderie.

Hospital de Bruma, though modest in size, marks a significant point on the Camino Inglés. Here, the modern-day pilgrim hospital continues the centuries-old tradition of providing refuge and care for travelers. This stop serves as a poignant reminder of the Camino's enduring spirit of hospitality and community, values that are deeply ingrained in the local way of life, encouraging a sense of gratitude and support among fellow pilgrims.

As pilgrims approach Santiago de Compostela, anticipation grows, culminating in the breathtaking view of the Cathedral of Santiago de Compostela. This architectural masterpiece symbolizes the end of the pilgrim's journey and serves as a treasure of art, history, and spirituality. The cathedral's Portico de la Gloria, the final embrace of Saint James, and the Pilgrim's Mass weave together the personal, cultural, and spiritual threads of the Camino, offering a transformative experience at the pilgrimage's conclusion. Throughout the Camino Inglés, opportunities to engage with Galicia's unique traditions arise in various forms. Sampling the local delicacy of pulpo a la gallega and participating in the communal ritual of the queimada, a traditional Galician punch, invite pilgrims to partake in customs that have been passed down through generations. These experiences enrich the journey and foster a deeper connection with the land and its people, encouraging a spirit of curiosity and appreciation.

The cultural stops along the Camino Inglés serve as gateways to understanding the rich tapestry of history, tradition, and community that defines this ancient pilgrimage route. Taking the time to explore these sites, engage with locals, and participate in traditions allows pilgrims to gain insights into the soul of Galicia and the timeless allure of the Camino de Santiago. This experience, while rooted in the past, offers lessons and reflections that resonate deeply with the modern pilgrim, making the Camino Inglés a truly transformative path.

CHAPTER 11: VIA DE LA PLATA

LONG DISTANCES AND HISTORIC PATHS

An example of the Camino de Santiago's enduring attraction is the Via de la Plata, an old road that has attracted innumerable pilgrims over the ages. This route, which runs more than 620 miles from Seville in southern Spain to Santiago de Compostela in northern Spain, is more than just a path; it is a journey through history, with each step echoing the footsteps of medieval pilgrims, Romans, and Moors. With roots in Roman times, it served as an essential north-south route that allowed troops, supplies, and information to be transported throughout the vast Iberian Peninsula. Today's pilgrims can experience a unique combination of challenge, tranquility, and a thorough exploration of Spain's rich history along the Via de la Plata.

The significance of the Via de la Plata in Camino history remains profound. It is the longest of all the Camino routes and traverses some of the most diverse landscapes Spain has to offer, from the arid plains of Extremadura to the lush greenery of Galicia. This route contrasts sharply with the more frequented Camino Francés, providing a sense of solitude and introspection that can be harder to find on the busier paths. The ancient Roman roads that form the backbone of this route constantly remind pilgrims of the millennia of history they are walking through. These roads, once the lifelines of the Roman Empire, now serve as pathways for spiritual seekers and adventurers, connecting the past with the present in a tangible, visceral way.

The historical context of the Via de la Plata enriches the pilgrimage experience. The route passes through ancient Roman cities like Mérida, known for its impressive aqueducts and amphitheaters, and Cáceres, whose old town is a UNESCO World Heritage Site. These cities provide pilgrims not just a place to rest but also a chance to step back in time and imagine life as it was thousands of years ago. The route also winds through territories once controlled by the Moors, adding layers of architectural and cultural diversity. The blend of Christian, Muslim, and Jewish heritage along the Via de la Plata vividly illustrates Spain's complex history of conquest and coexistence.

Figure 19. Roman Bride in Mérida

Pilgrims walking the Via de la Plata face unique challenges due to the long distances between towns and the sparse population in certain areas, which require careful planning. The solitude of the route, while one of its most appealing features, necessitates self-reliance and preparation. Carrying sufficient water, especially in the hotter months, and being aware of the distances between accommodations are essential. Despite these challenges, walking the Via de la Plata offers immense rewards. The route provides a sense of peace and space for reflection that is harder to find on the more crowded Camino paths. Completing Spain's longest Camino route, combined with deep historical and cultural immersion, creates a profoundly transformative experience.

For those drawn to the Via de la Plata, this pilgrimage represents more than a simple trek; it serves as a passage through the heart of Spain's history, along roads built by Romans, trodden by medieval pilgrims, and now walked by modern-day seekers. The ancient origins of this route, its connection to Roman roads, and its significance in Camino history transform academic facts into lived experiences, felt with every step along this historic path. The Via de la Plata presents a unique opportunity to connect with the past, challenge oneself physically and spiritually, and experience the transformative power of the Camino de Santiago.

Daily Stages and Unique Challenges

Pilgrims on the Via de la Plata face a series of daily stages that challenge their endurance, resilience, and preparation. The long distances between populated areas and the limited availability of water sources create unique obstacles that demand strategic planning and adaptability. To navigate these challenges successfully, it is crucial to understand the specifics of each stage and prepare for the environmental conditions encountered along the way.

The initial stages from Seville to Mérida feature relatively flat terrain but expose pilgrims to the intense Spanish sun, especially during the summer months when temperatures can exceed 35°C (95°F). During these stages, carrying at least 2 liters of water is advisable, as opportunities for replenishment are often limited to small villages encountered sporadically along the route. Sun protection, including a wide-brimmed hat, high SPF sunscreen, and lightweight, long-sleeved clothing, becomes essential to prevent heatstroke and sunburn. Taking these precautions keeps you safe and enhances your overall experience.

As the Via de la Plata progresses northward, the landscape begins to undulate, introducing more challenging terrains in the provinces of Castilla y León and, eventually, Galicia. The stages between Zamora and Ourense feature a mix of steep ascents and descents, which can strain the knees and require a slower pace. For these sections, using trekking poles proves beneficial, offering additional stability and reducing the impact on joints. Connecting with the rhythm of these changes can deepen your experience.

The approach to Galicia brings a significant shift in environmental conditions. The region's notorious rainfall requires waterproof gear, including a reliable rain jacket, pack cover, and quick-drying clothing. Despite the potential for wet conditions, the beauty of the lush, green landscapes provides a rewarding backdrop that contrasts sharply with the arid expanses of Extremadura. This transformation serves as a refreshing reminder of nature's diversity.

It is crucial to divide the Via de la Plata into manageable daily stages due to its length and the diverse terrain it traverses. Most people can maintain a sustainable pace of 20 to 25 kilometers (12 to 15 miles) per day, which allows for rest periods and touring the towns and villages along the way. However, some stages, particularly in the less populated southern sections, may require covering distances of up to 30 kilometers (about 18 miles) to reach the next available accommodation. In these cases, starting the day's walk early to avoid the midday heat and planning for a longer rest period upon arrival can help manage fatigue. This thoughtful approach enhances the experience and makes the trek feel more enjoyable.

Accommodations along the Via de la Plata are less frequent than on the more traveled Camino Francés, making booking necessary in some areas, especially during peak pilgrimage and tourist seasons. A guidebook or app that provides up-to-date contact information for albergues and guesthouses is invaluable for securing nightly stays. Carrying a lightweight tent or bivvy bag offers an alternative for the more adventurous pilgrims, granting flexibility while requiring careful consideration of camping regulations in Spain. Being prepared in this way ensures a roof over your head and opens up new possibilities for your experience.

Water sources along the Via de la Plata, while generally reliable in towns and villages, can be scarce in the more remote stretches. Pilgrims should meticulously plan their daily water needs, refilling at every opportunity and using water purification tablets or filters when the quality of the source is uncertain. Snacks and energy-rich foods are also essential provisions, as dining options may be limited outside of the main population centers. A little foresight in these areas significantly impacts comfort and energy levels.

The pilgrim's determination and flexibility are put to the test by the particular difficulties of the Via de la Plata, which include difficult distances, adverse winters, and irregular terrain. Pilgrims can overcome these obstacles and find chances for introspection and personal development if they prepare well and approach each day's journey with awareness. This historic route's beauty and seclusion provide a very intimate pilgrimage experience, enhanced by the natural beauty and history of the places it passes through.

Why This Route Stands Out

The Via de la Plata distinguishes itself as a unique pilgrimage route that offers a blend of solitude, rich cultural heritage, and the rewarding experience of traversing Spain's longest Camino path. Unlike the more frequented Camino Francés, the Via de la Plata provides a route through the heart of Spain that is both physically challenging and spiritually enriching. This path stands out for several reasons, each contributing to a deeply personal and transformative pilgrimage experience.

Solitude serves as one of the Via de la Plata's most compelling features. Many pilgrims find the opportunity to walk in quiet reflection, away from the crowds, to be a powerful draw. This solitude fosters a more introspective experience, where the physical act of walking becomes a meditative practice. Pilgrims immerse themselves in the natural beauty and silence of the Spanish countryside, which offers a sense of peace and space for personal growth. The less trodden path also creates a unique sense of camaraderie among those who choose this route, leading to meaningful connections with fellow pilgrims that can be both uplifting and inspiring.

The rich cultural heritage encountered along the Via de la Plata is unparalleled. The route passes through regions steeped in history, from the ancient Roman city of Mérida to the medieval streets of Salamanca. Each town and village along the way tells a story, providing pilgrims with a living history lesson. The architectural marvels, from Roman aqueducts to Gothic cathedrals, serve as waypoints on a journey through Spain's diverse cultural landscape. The route's passage through territories once under Moorish control adds a layer of complexity to the pilgrimage, as Islamic, Jewish, and Christian influences intermingle, creating a rich tapestry of Spain's historical narrative that encourages curiosity and exploration.

Completing Spain's longest Camino route offers a rewarding experience that cannot be overstated. Covering over 1,000 kilometers, the Via de la Plata challenges pilgrims not just physically but mentally and spiritually. The sense of achievement upon reaching Santiago de Compostela magnifies with the knowledge of the distance traveled and the obstacles overcome. This route tests the pilgrim's resolve, endurance, and faith, making the arrival in Santiago all the more triumphant. The path along the Via de la Plata reveals the depths of one's strength and resilience while exploring the landscape of Spain, reminding pilgrims of their capability to achieve great things.

For those seeking a pilgrimage that combines the challenge of long-distance walking with opportunities for deep personal reflection and cultural immersion, the Via de la Plata is unmatched. Its solitude provides a break from the noise of everyday life, allowing pilgrims to listen to their thoughts and the world around them. The rich cultural heritage of the regions it passes through enhances the experience, turning each step into a discovery. Completing such a formidable route leaves pilgrims with a profound sense of accomplishment and transformation. The Via de la Plata stands out not just as a path to Santiago but as a profound exploration of the soul of Spain and the heart of the pilgrim.

Camino Sanabrés: A Direct Route to Santiago

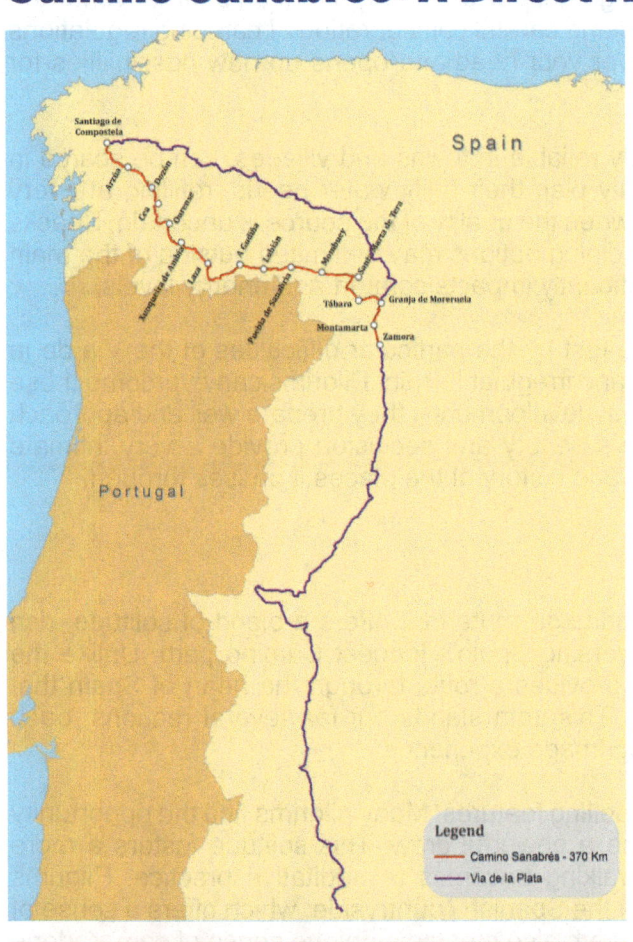

An alternative for those looking to streamline their journey is the Camino Sanabrés, a direct route from the Via de la Plata that bypasses the detour through Astorga. This path offers a more straightforward approach to Santiago, allowing pilgrims to maintain their focus on the pilgrimage's spiritual and personal aspects without the added complexity of longer diversions. The Camino Sanabrés retains the essence of the Via de la Plata, providing opportunities for reflection and cultural engagement while ensuring a more efficient journey to the sacred city.

Pilgrims on this route can still experience the beauty of the Spanish landscape and the rich history of the towns they pass through, all while enjoying the satisfaction of a direct path to their destination. The Camino Sanabrés is not just a shortcut; it is a thoughtfully designed pilgrimage that encourages a deeper connection with the journey itself. As you walk, you will encounter charming villages, ancient churches, and breathtaking vistas that remind you of the rich tapestry of life along the Camino.

This route allows for moments of introspection, where the simplicity of walking can lead to profound insights. The directness of the Camino Sanabrés does not diminish the spiritual experience; rather, it enhances it by allowing pilgrims to engage more fully with their thoughts and surroundings. Each step taken on this path is a step toward not only Santiago but also personal growth and understanding.

For those who may feel overwhelmed by the longer distances of the Via de la Plata, the Camino Sanabrés offers a reassuring alternative that still embodies the spirit of pilgrimage. It invites you to embrace the journey, savor the moments of quiet reflection, and connect with the rich cultural heritage of Spain. Completing this route provides a sense of accomplishment and fulfillment as you arrive in Santiago with a heart full of memories and a spirit renewed by the experience.

CHAPTER 12: BEYOND SANTIAGO

WALKING TO THE END OF THE WORLD

The tradition of continuing the pilgrimage beyond Santiago de Compostela to Finisterre and Muxía holds a blend of historical, spiritual, and cultural significance that resonates deeply with many pilgrims. This extension of the journey encapsulates a quest for a more profound sense of closure and personal fulfillment, often described as walking to the "End of the World."

Finisterre, derived from the Latin "Finis Terrae," meaning "End of the Earth," was believed by the Romans to be the westernmost point of the known world. A potent symbol of life's journey and the mysteries that remain beyond our comprehension is created by the rocky coastline and the vast Atlantic Ocean beyond. When pilgrims arrive at Finisterre, they have the chance to pause and think deeply about the journey's influence on their lives and the opportunities that lie ahead.

Muxía is known for its serene beauty and the Sanctuary of Nuestra Señora de la Barca, a place shrouded in legends of the Virgin Mary's arrival by boat to comfort Saint James. The spiritual ambiance of Muxía, combined with the natural beauty of its coastal setting, provides a tranquil space for pilgrims to meditate on their experiences and the transformative nature of their journey.

Figure 23. Sanctuary of Nuestra Señora de la Barca

Continuing to Finisterre and Muxía often serves as the final leg of a transformative pilgrimage, offering a space for closure and reflection. Pilgrims are drawn to these destinations for the physical challenge and the symbolic act of casting off the old while embracing renewal. It is a tradition for pilgrims to burn worn-out clothes or boots at Finisterre, symbolizing the shedding of personal burdens and the beginning of a new chapter in their lives, encouraging a fresh start filled with hope.

The spiritual significance of this extension remains deeply personal, with many pilgrims reporting a sense of completion and peace upon reaching these final destinations. The trek to Finisterre and Muxía allows for a transition from the Camino's communal spirit back to the individual's daily life, enriched by the lessons and experiences gained along the way.

Because these locations are rich in centuries of pilgrimage history, local folklore, and customs that enhance the pilgrim's experience, cultural significance is crucial. The locals' warmth, the cuisine of the area, and the breathtaking scenery all combine to make the pilgrimage's conclusion unforgettable and significant.

Those planning to extend their journey to Finisterre and Muxía should consider the practical aspects of this additional trek. The distance from Santiago to Finisterre is approximately 90 kilometers (about 56 miles), and from there to Muxía, an additional 30 kilometers (about 19 miles). Pilgrims should plan for an average of three to four days of walking to reach Finisterre and an additional day to reach Muxía. Accommodations along these routes include albergues, guesthouses, and hotels, catering to the needs of pilgrims seeking rest and reflection.

Similar to the original Camino journey, preparation for this extension includes packing weather-appropriate clothing, making sure you have the right shoes, and keeping an eye on your nutrition and hydration. The paths are well-marked, with the familiar yellow arrows and scallop shells guiding pilgrims to their final destinations, assuring them that they are on the right track.

The trek to Finisterre and Muxía represents a significant spiritual and cultural extension of the Camino de Santiago. It offers pilgrims a unique opportunity to reflect on their pilgrimage, engage with ancient traditions, and experience a sense of renewal and completion. This final leg of the journey stands as a testament to the enduring allure of the Camino, inviting pilgrims to explore the depths of their spirit against the backdrop of Spain's breathtaking landscapes.

Coastal Reflections and Stunning Views

Every step of the journey from Santiago to Finisterre and Muxía exhibits the natural beauty that defines this extension, revealing a tapestry of beautiful landscapes and rocky coastlines. As the landscape changes to reveal the amazing natural, unadulterated beauty of Galicia's coast, pilgrims move westward. The route offers expansive views that make up for the difficulties encountered along the way as it winds through forests, alongside cliffs, and past remote beaches.

Figure 24. Muxía

Stunning views define this route, with the vast expanse of the Atlantic Ocean stretching to the horizon. Sunsets here mesmerize, painting the sky in vibrant hues as the sun sinks below the ocean—a spectacle that many pilgrims take time to witness. These moments of natural beauty foster a profound sense of peace and reflection, enhancing the spiritual and emotional impact of the pilgrimage.

The serene atmosphere of the coastal path stands in contrast to the more traveled routes to Santiago. The sound of waves crashing against the cliffs, the scent of salt in the air, and the gentle breeze create a meditative backdrop that encourages introspection and connection with nature. This tranquility soothes the soul, providing a nurturing space for pilgrims to contemplate their experiences and the transformations inspired within them.

Rugged coastlines along the way vividly remind travelers of nature's power and beauty. Rocky outcrops, hidden coves, and the occasional lighthouse enhance the sense of adventure and discovery. Navigating this terrain requires mindfulness and respect for the natural environment, reinforcing the pilgrimage's ethos The addition of Finisterre and Muxía is particularly noteworthy for individuals looking for a life-changing Camino experience. In addition to being physically demanding, it allows pilgrims to travel through some of Spain's most breathtaking coastal landscapes, allowing them to delve deeply within themselves while listening to the ocean's timeless rhythm. The last section of the Camino de Santiago is a remarkable journey of exploration because of its exceptional combination of natural beauty, tranquil surroundings, and rough terrain.

Practical Tips for This Optional Route

For those planning to extend their pilgrimage to Finisterre and Muxía, grasping the practicalities of this route is crucial for a seamless experience. The distance from Santiago to Finisterre measures approximately 90 kilometers (56 miles), and the trip typically takes three to four days to complete. Pilgrims then face an additional 30 kilometers (19 miles) from Finisterre to Muxía, usually covered in one day. Given these distances, pacing is essential, along with planning for overnight stays. Accommodations along this stretch include albergues, guesthouses, and hotels, each offering varying levels of comfort and amenities. Booking early is advisable, especially during peak pilgrimage seasons, to secure preferred lodging options and ensure a restful night's sleep.

Trail conditions on the way to Finisterre and Muxía can be challenging, featuring varied terrain such as coastal paths, forested areas, and occasional steep climbs. Weather significantly impacts trail conditions, with fog and rain common in Galicia. Pilgrims should pack waterproof gear and prepare for sudden weather changes, as readiness for the unexpected can greatly enhance the experience. Footwear with good grip and support is essential for safely navigating slippery or rocky sections, instilling confidence to tackle the path ahead.

Transportation options for returning to Santiago from Finisterre or Muxía are well-organized due to the popularity of these routes. Regular bus services connect these towns with Santiago, providing convenient travel back to the city. Schedules may vary seasonally, so checking the latest timetables in advance is wise. For those seeking more flexibility, taxi services are also available, although they can be a more costly option. Pilgrims returning to Santiago for their onward journey or flight home should allow ample time for travel from these coastal destinations to ensure a smooth transition back.

When planning accommodations, consider the unique characteristics of each town along the route. In Finisterre, many establishments cater to pilgrims, offering communal dining options and spaces for reflection and camaraderie. Muxía, while smaller, provides a tranquil setting with several intimate guesthouses and albergues that emphasize personal service and comfort. Both towns have amenities that cater to pilgrims' needs, such as laundry and drying rooms, safe backpack storage, and adjustable check-in hours to suit walking schedules, guaranteeing a comfortable stay.

Dining along the route presents an opportunity to savor local Galician cuisine, known for its seafood and hearty dishes. Many restaurants and cafes in Finisterre and Muxía take pride in serving traditional meals that reflect the region's culinary heritage. Pilgrims can enjoy dishes such as pulpo a la gallega (octopus), empanadas (savory pies), and caldo gallego (a Galician soup), providing nourishing and comforting meals after a day of walking. Budget-friendly options are available, with many establishments offering pilgrim menus at a fixed price that includes a starter, main course, dessert, and beverage, ensuring a satisfying meal without straining your budget.

Planning for the extension to Finisterre and Muxía involves thoughtful preparation, from selecting appropriate gear to accommodate the varied terrain and weather conditions to arranging accommodations and meals that enhance the pilgrimage experience. Considering these practical tips allows pilgrims to enjoy a fulfilling conclusion to their Camino, marked by reflection, renewal, and the breathtaking beauty of Spain's western coast.

PART III: WALKING THE CAMINO

CHAPTER 13: NAVIGATING THE CAMINO CONFIDENTLY

• • • • •

FOLLOWING WAYMARKS: ARROWS, SHELLS, SIGNS

Navigating the Camino de Santiago relies heavily on an age-old system of waymarks consisting of yellow arrows, scallop shells, and various signs. These symbols serve as the pilgrims' compass, guiding them through diverse terrains and ensuring they remain on the correct path to Santiago de Compostela. Knowing how to follow these waymarks is crucial for a stress-free experience, allowing pilgrims to focus on the spiritual and personal growth aspects of their pilgrimage.

Yellow arrows are the most ubiquitous markers along the Camino. Painted on trees, stones, sidewalks, and even urban walls, these arrows point in the direction of travel. The simplicity of the yellow arrow system means that even in remote areas, where signage might be sparse, the next arrow is rarely too far ahead. Pilgrims should watch for these arrows, especially at intersections or where the path might not be immediately clear. In urban areas, arrows can sometimes be found at higher elevations, like the sides of buildings, so looking up occasionally and staying engaged with your surroundings is beneficial.

Scallop shells carry deep historical and spiritual significance for the Camino, symbolizing the journey of the pilgrim. The lines on the shell represent the various paths that pilgrims travel from all over the world, all converging at a single point: the tomb of Saint James in Santiago. These shells serve as a motif on official Camino signs and are physically attached to paths, buildings, and milestones. The direction of the shell's grooves indicates the forward direction, guiding pilgrims along the correct path with a sense of purpose.

Signs along the Camino can vary significantly depending on the region. They might include municipal signs, official Camino de Santiago markers, and informational boards. These signs often provide additional context about the distance to the next town, historical information, or directions to nearby points of interest. While not as uniformly present as yellow arrows and scallop shells, these signs offer valuable insights and reassurance about the journey ahead, helping you feel more connected to the path.

To avoid getting lost, pilgrims should maintain a steady pace and stay vigilant for these markers, especially when leaving towns or crossing through farmlands where the path might not be as well-trodden. If you reach a fork without a clear marker in sight, it's wise to backtrack to the last known waymark to reassess your direction. This simple step can help you regain confidence in your journey.

Local knowledge becomes invaluable in the unlikely scenario that waymarks appear to be missing or vandalized. Asking fellow pilgrims or locals for directions is a good practice. The Camino de Santiago is well-traveled, and the people living along the route are generally familiar with the way and eager to assist pilgrims in finding their way, creating a sense of community and support.

For additional peace of mind, technology can serve as a supplementary navigation tool. GPS devices and smartphone apps dedicated to the Camino offer digital maps and route information that can confirm you're on the right path. However, balancing reliance on electronic devices with the traditional waymarking system enhances your engagement with the Camino experience and the world around you.

Familiarity with these symbols and their meanings equips you to follow the Camino's path through Spain's breathtaking landscapes. The waymarks serve not just as navigational tools but also embody the collective spirit of millions of pilgrims who have walked the path before, offering guidance, reassurance, and a sense of belonging to a community that spans centuries.

Using Apps for Stress-Free Walking

In the digital age, modern technology enhances the traditional pilgrimage of the Camino de Santiago, providing pilgrims with innovative tools. This section explores apps and tools designed to facilitate stress-free walking, allowing pilgrims to navigate the Camino with confidence and ease. These digital companions serve as a backup to physical waymarks while enriching the pilgrimage with detailed information on routes, accommodations, and cultural sites.

A reliable GPS navigation app specifically tailored for the Camino de Santiago stands out as one of the most valuable assets for any pilgrim. Apps like "Camino Pilgrim - Frances and "Buen Camino" have become essential for many walkers. These apps feature detailed maps of routes, including the Camino Francés and Camino Portugués, pinpointing the locations of albergues, restaurants, and points of interest. They offer real-time GPS tracking to keep you on the correct path and provide alternative routes in case of detours or personal preferences. The interactive nature of these apps allows for updates on trail conditions, weather forecasts, and social features to connect with fellow pilgrims, fostering a sense of community along the way.

Accommodation booking apps also play a crucial role. Platforms like Booking.com and Hostelworld include sections dedicated to the Camino, showcasing pilgrim-friendly lodging options. These apps enable users to filter based on budget, location, and amenities, simplifying the process of planning stays in advance or finding last-minute accommodations. Reading reviews from fellow pilgrims offers insight into the quality of the stays and what to expect upon arrival, helping you feel better prepared and at ease.

For those interested in the cultural and historical aspects of the Camino, apps like "Camino de Santiago Companion" provide a wealth of information on landmarks, churches, and historical sites encountered along the way. This app acts as a digital guidebook, enriching the pilgrimage experience with background stories and details that might otherwise be missed, adding depth to your exploration.

Language barriers can pose challenges for many pilgrims, especially in remote areas of the Camino where English may not be widely spoken. Translation apps such as Google Translate, featuring a camera for instant translation of menus, signs, and information boards, can significantly ease communication. Having a basic Spanish phrasebook app facilitates more personal interactions with locals and fellow pilgrims, enhancing the social aspect of the Camino and making it more enjoyable.

A comprehensive fitness and tracking app proves invaluable for preparing for the Camino and monitoring progress along the way. Apps like Strava or MapMyWalk track daily distances, steps, and calories burned while allowing pilgrims to share their experiences with friends and family back home. This feature reassures solo travelers and their loved ones, providing a sense of safety and connection despite the physical distance. Integrating these apps and tools into your Camino planning and daily routine significantly reduces the stress of navigation, accommodation booking, and communication. Pilgrims can concentrate more on the spiritual, individual, and cultural exploration that the Camino de Santiago offers by utilizing technology. It's essential to balance the use of digital tools with opportunities to disconnect and fully immerse yourself in the experience. Remember to engage with fellow pilgrims and let the Camino's timeless path guide you both physically and spiritually.

Avoiding Common Navigation Mistakes

One common mistake pilgrims make on the Camino de Santiago is relying too heavily on physical markers without having a backup plan. While the yellow arrows and scallop shells serve as reliable guides, construction, seasonal changes, or even vandalism can sometimes obscure these markers. Always carry a current guidebook or map of your route. These resources provide valuable context to the waymarks and offer alternative paths or detours that might not be immediately apparent from the trail markers alone. Making plans for different daylight hours is another common mistake. The number of hours you have to walk each day can be affected by the substantial variations in daylight throughout the year. Starting your day early guarantees that you avoid navigating in the dark and helps you maximize the daylight, particularly on shorter days. This is crucial for safety because after sunset, visibility deteriorates, and it becomes more likely that waymarks will be missed.

Ignoring weather forecasts can lead to discomfort or even danger. Weather conditions can change rapidly, especially in mountainous areas along the Camino. Check the forecast daily and prepare with the appropriate gear. Sudden rain can make the path slippery and obscure trail markers. A lightweight, waterproof jacket and cover for your backpack are essential items to include in your preparation.

Underestimating the importance of hydration and nutrition can detract from your Camino experience. While many towns along the route offer readily available food and water, some stretches can be scarce in resources. Always carry water and snacks to maintain your energy levels, particularly on more remote parts of the trail. Staying well-hydrated and fueled helps you avoid fatigue, making it easier to stay focused and oriented.

Overpacking often leads to physical strain and fatigue, making it harder to stay alert and oriented. Review your pack list critically, focusing on essentials and leaving behind items you can do without. A lighter pack enables you to move more freely, reducing the risk of injury and keeping your mind clear for navigation rather than discomfort.

Engaging with the pilgrim community opens up opportunities for valuable insights and advice. Fellow pilgrims can provide real-time information about the route ahead, including potential navigational challenges. Sharing experiences in the evening at albergues or during rest stops keeps you informed about any recent changes in the path or offers helpful tips for navigating tricky sections.

Being mindful of these common mistakes and adopting a proactive, prepared approach to your pilgrimage allows you to navigate the Camino de Santiago with confidence and ease. Remember, the experience is not just about reaching Santiago but about appreciating each step of the path with awareness and intention.

CHAPTER 14: SAFE, COMFORTABLE, AND PREPARED

SAFETY TIPS FOR VULNERABLE PILGRIMS

For women, solo walkers, and older pilgrims on the Camino de Santiago, safety and comfort hold great importance. These groups often encounter unique challenges, but with effective strategies, the experience can be both empowering and fulfilling. The following tips address specific concerns, promoting a safe and comfortable pilgrimage.

Safety Strategies for Women: Female pilgrims, particularly those traveling alone, should prioritize safety by choosing well-reviewed accommodations that cater to solo travelers. Many albergues provide female-only dorms or private rooms, creating a sense of security and community. Sharing plans with family or friends, including accommodation details and daily check-ins, can also enhance peace of mind. Joining a Camino forum or social media group enables connections with fellow female pilgrims. These platforms serve as valuable resources for sharing experiences and arranging meet-ups, fostering a supportive network.

Smart Route Choices for Solo Walkers: Solo pilgrims, regardless of gender, benefit from selecting popular routes like the Camino Francés, which are well-traveled and marked. This reduces the risk of getting lost and ensures a supportive pilgrim community is nearby. Carrying a whistle and a charged phone with emergency numbers saved creates a safety net in case of emergencies. Solo walkers should trust their intuition; if a situation feels unsafe, it is wise to remove oneself from it.

Confidence-Boosting Tips for Older Pilgrims: Older pilgrims might have concerns about their physical ability to complete the Camino. However, many find the experience incredibly rewarding with the right preparation. Selecting a route that aligns with one's physical capability is crucial; the Camino Portugués, for instance, offers flatter terrain and shorter stages. Engaging in a fitness regimen tailored to walking long distances builds both strength and confidence. Older pilgrims should also consider packing lightweight gear to minimize strain and possibly using a luggage transfer service to ease the physical burden of carrying a backpack daily.

General Safety Tips: All vulnerable travelers should familiarize themselves with the terrain and typical weather conditions of their chosen route to pack appropriately and avoid surprises. Wearing reflective gear and using a headlamp prove beneficial for early morning or late evening walks. Keeping valuables secure and close to the body, in a money belt or a secure pocket, helps prevent theft.

Health and Comfort: Staying hydrated and nourished is vital. Carrying water and snacks, along with knowing the locations of towns or villages to replenish supplies, is essential. Comfortable, broken-in footwear and moisture-wicking clothing prevent blisters and discomfort, ensuring a more enjoyable experience. Regularly applying sunscreen and wearing a hat protects against sunburn, a common issue for pilgrims.

Engaging with the Pilgrim Community: The Camino is renowned for its spirit of camaraderie. Interacting with other pilgrims enhances the experience and provides a network of support. Many pilgrims form lifelong friendships along the Camino. Participating in communal dinners at albergues and attending pilgrim masses enriches the experience with shared moments and insights.

Women, solo walkers, and older pilgrims can navigate the Camino de Santiago with confidence by implementing these strategies. This path offers a unique opportunity for personal growth, reflection, and connection with a diverse community of travelers. With careful planning and a proactive approach to safety and comfort, the Camino can transform the experience for pilgrims of all backgrounds and ages.

Walking with Your Dog

Taking your dog along the Camino de Santiago adds a unique layer of companionship and challenge to your pilgrimage. To ensure a seamless experience for both you and your furry friend, meticulous planning is essential. Consider pet-friendly accommodations, route-specific challenges, vet access, and best practices for a harmonious trip.

Pet-Friendly Accommodations: Not all albergues and hotels on the Camino welcome pets. Before you set out, compile a list of accommodations that allow pets, including private rooms in hostels, guesthouses, and campsites where you and your dog can rest comfortably. Platforms like Booking.com often provide filters for pet-friendly options. Always confirm directly with the property about their pet policy to avoid surprises. Some places may require a pet deposit or have specific rooms designated for pilgrims with pets, so early booking is crucial for a smooth stay.

Route-Specific Challenges: The Camino de Santiago features diverse terrains, from paved roads to rugged mountain paths. Assess the physical demands of the route on your dog, especially on more challenging trails like the Camino Primitivo or parts of the Camino del Norte. Protect your dog's paws with appropriate booties if you anticipate rough terrain, and carry enough water for both of you, as some stretches may have limited access to fresh water. Be aware of the weather conditions, particularly during the summer months, to prevent heatstroke and keep your furry companion comfortable.

Vet Access: Familiarize yourself with the locations of veterinary clinics along your chosen route. Keep a list of contacts for vets in major towns and cities you will pass through. Apps like Google Maps or local Camino forums can help you find vet services. Ensure your dog is up-to-date on vaccinations and carry a health certificate along with any medications they may need. It's wise to have a basic pet first aid kit for minor injuries your dog might sustain on the trail, as being prepared can make a significant difference.

Best Practices: Keeping your dog on a leash is fundamental on the Camino, ensuring their safety and respecting other pilgrims and local wildlife. Always clean up after your dog and carry enough waste bags for this purpose. Feeding your dog a consistent diet can be challenging on the Camino, so pack a supply of their regular food to avoid gastrointestinal issues. Hydration is crucial for your dog as well as for you, so plan your stages with water sources in mind to keep both of you refreshed.

Socializing your dog for the trip is essential. The Camino will expose your dog to crowds, other animals, and new environments. Ensuring they behave well and feel comfortable with these interactions will enhance the experience for everyone involved.

Respect the Camino's ethos and the local environment by keeping your dog under control and minimizing their impact on nature and the communities you visit. This respect includes recognizing when your dog may need a rest day or a shorter walking stage, as their endurance will dictate your pace and overall enjoyment of the experience.

Walking the Camino with your dog requires additional preparation and consideration, but it can be an immensely rewarding experience. Focus on pet-friendly accommodations, prepare for the route's physical demands, ensure access to veterinary care, and adhere to best practices for traveling with pets to create a memorable pilgrimage that strengthens the bond between you and your dog.

Emergency Actions on the Camino

In the event of an emergency on the Camino de Santiago, being prepared and knowing the appropriate steps to take can significantly impact the outcome. Whether facing injuries, getting lost, theft, or requiring assistance in remote or urban areas, a clear action plan is essential for every pilgrim. This section provides a detailed, step-by-step guide to managing emergencies, ensuring pilgrims can navigate these challenges with confidence and safety.

Injuries: If you or a fellow pilgrim sustains an injury, first assess the severity. For minor injuries such as cuts, scrapes, or blisters, clean the wound with antiseptic wipes and apply a sterile bandage. Always carry a basic first aid kit for such instances. For more serious injuries, do not move the injured person unless they are in immediate danger. Call the emergency services number in Spain, 112, and provide them with your exact location and a description of the injury. If you are in a remote area, use a whistle or an emergency beacon to signal for help. Having basic knowledge of first aid and CPR before starting your Camino can empower you to act effectively.

Getting Lost: If you find yourself off the marked Camino path, remain calm. Stay where you are to avoid getting further lost. Use your phone's GPS to determine your location and try to retrace your steps back to the last known waymark. If you're unable to find your way back, call 112 and provide them with your location. Carry a physical map and a compass as backups for electronic devices. Informing someone of your daily route plan can also be invaluable in such situations, as they can raise the alarm if you do not check in as expected.

Theft: While the Camino is generally safe, theft can occur. If you become a victim of theft, report the incident to the nearest police station as soon as possible. Keep a separate record of important documents like your passport, credit card, and insurance information, both physically and digitally, so you can access them if the originals are stolen. Using money belts or hidden pouches for valuables can reduce the risk of theft. Be particularly vigilant in crowded areas and avoid displaying expensive equipment or jewelry openly; staying alert can help you feel more at ease.

Seeking Help on Remote or Urban Trails: In remote areas, pilgrim shelters (albergues) and local businesses serve as valuable resources for assistance. They can provide or call for transportation, medical services, or law enforcement if needed. In urban areas, besides the police, you can seek help from tourist information centers, pharmacies, and hospitals. Always carry a list of essential contacts, including local emergency services, the nearest embassy or consulate, and taxi services. Learning basic Spanish phrases for emergencies or having a translation app can facilitate communication in critical situations, making it easier to get the help you need.

General Preparedness: Carry a charged mobile phone with a local SIM card or international roaming to ensure you can make calls in an emergency. Download offline maps and emergency apps before starting your Camino, as these can be lifesaving. Joining a Camino pilgrim group online provides a network of support where you can share your location and find assistance from fellow pilgrims.

Preparing for emergencies and knowing the steps to take allows pilgrims to address challenges more effectively, ensuring a safer and more secure Camino experience. The Camino de Santiago fosters a community of support, where help is often at hand from fellow pilgrims and residents alike.

CHAPTER 15: ACCOMMODATIONS AND DINING

CHOOSING THE RIGHT ACCOMMODATION

Choosing the right accommodation along the Camino de Santiago plays a crucial role in ensuring a restful and rejuvenating experience. The Camino offers a variety of lodging options that cater to different needs, preferences and budgets. Knowing the differences between albergues, hotels and guesthouses will help you make informed decisions that align with your pilgrimage, contributing to a memorable experience.

Albergues serve as the most traditional form of accommodation on the Camino, specifically designed for pilgrims. They include municipal albergues, often the most economical choice, and private albergues that may offer additional amenities at a slightly higher cost. Albergues create a communal living experience with dormitory-style sleeping arrangements, shared bathrooms, and communal kitchen facilities. This environment fosters a unique camaraderie among pilgrims, providing opportunities to meet and bond with fellow travelers from around the world. For those seeking an authentic pilgrim experience or traveling on a tighter budget, albergues are an excellent option. However, privacy is limited, and amenities such as laundry services or Wi-Fi can vary greatly. Many albergues operate on a first-come, first-served basis, which can introduce uncertainty during peak pilgrimage seasons.

Hotels on the Camino offer a more private and comfortable lodging option. They range from basic, family-run establishments to luxurious hotels with a wide array of amenities, including private bathrooms, on-site dining, and sometimes even spa facilities. Hotels suit those seeking solitude and comfort or who may be walking the Camino as part of a vacation rather than a traditional pilgrimage. The cost of hotels is significantly higher than that of albergues, but many find the added comfort and amenities justify the extra expense. Booking in advance is highly recommended, especially in smaller towns where options may be limited.

Guesthouses, or "pensiones," provide a middle ground between the communal atmosphere of albergues and the privacy of hotels. These family-run accommodations are often more intimate, with fewer rooms than hotels, creating a cozy and personal experience. Guesthouses typically offer private or shared rooms at a moderate price point, making them a viable option for those who desire privacy without the higher cost of a hotel. Many guesthouses also provide breakfast or have a small restaurant on-site, enhancing convenience. When selecting the right stay, consider the following factors:

1. Comfort vs. Cost: Determine your budget and the level of comfort you require. If you are willing to sacrifice some comfort for a more immersive pilgrim experience and lower cost, albergues are the best choice. For those who prioritize privacy and amenities, hotels or guesthouses may be more suitable.

2. Amenities: Assess which amenities are essential for your journey. Wi-Fi, laundry services, and on-site dining can significantly enhance your experience but may come at a higher cost.

3. Location: Consider the location of your accommodation relative to the Camino route. Staying closer to the trail can save time and energy, but options may be more limited and expensive.

4. Social Experience: Reflect on the level of social interaction you desire. Albergues provide a communal environment conducive to making connections, while hotels and guesthouses offer a more secluded experience.

5-Reservations: During peak seasons, booking accommodations in advance can alleviate stress and ensure you have a place to rest each night. This is especially important for hotels and guesthouses, which may fill up quickly.

Carefully considering these factors allows you to choose accommodations that meet your needs and enhance your Camino experience. Whether you select the communal spirit of an albergue, the comfort of a hotel, or the charm of a guesthouse, each option offers a unique way to experience the Camino de Santiago. The right choice reflects your individual preferences, ensuring a fulfilling and memorable pilgrimage.

Choosing the right accommodation along the Camino de Santiago plays a crucial role in ensuring a restful and rejuvenating experience. The Camino offers a variety of lodging options that cater to different needs, prefeCamino Meal Customs

The meal customs along the Camino de Santiago go beyond merely nourishing the body; they play a vital role in the pilgrimage experience, offering insights into local culture and creating opportunities for connection with fellow pilgrims. Communal dining, a common practice in many albergues, serves as a foundation of Camino culture. This tradition fosters a sense of community and shared experience among travelers from various backgrounds. Communal meals typically feature a pilgrim menu, a fixed-price offering that includes a starter, main course, dessert, and sometimes a drink, providing substantial nourishment at an affordable price.

Pilgrim menus are carefully crafted to meet the needs of walkers, delivering a balanced combination of carbohydrates, proteins, and fats to refuel after a long day of hiking. Starters may include local soups like Caldo Gallego in Galicia, a hearty broth made with greens, potatoes, and chorizo, or a simple mixed salad with tuna. Main course options often highlight regional specialties such as Pulpo a la Gallega, tender octopus seasoned with paprika and olive oil, or a hearty plate of Lentejas, lentil stew with chorizo, a staple across Spain. Desserts typically consist of simple choices like Flan, a caramel custard, or Arroz con Leche, a creamy rice pudding. These meals provide essential sustenance while introducing pilgrims to the rich tapestry of Spanish cuisine.

Eating like a local involves adapting to the Spanish dining schedule, which generally includes a light breakfast, a substantial lunch—the main meal of the day, enjoyed between 1:00 and 3:00 PM—and a lighter dinner, served from 8:00 PM onwards. This schedule may require some adjustment, but it aligns well with the walking rhythm of the Camino, allowing pilgrims to start their day early, enjoy a significant midday meal, and conclude with a communal dinner after reaching their evening destination.

Must-try dishes along the Camino vary by region but generally feature Tortilla Española, a thick potato omelet found throughout Spain; Paella in its many regional variations, especially when passing through Valencia; and Galicia Empanadas, savory pastries filled with meat or seafood. Sampling these dishes offers not only a taste of Spain's culinary diversity but also a deeper connection to the places and people encountered along the way.

For those with dietary restrictions or preferences, many establishments along the Camino are becoming more accommodating, providing vegetarian, vegan, and gluten-free options. Communicating your needs in Spanish or carrying a dietary restriction card in Spanish can help ensure an enjoyable communal dining experience without compromise.

The meal customs on the Camino de Santiago encompass nourishment, cultural immersion, and community building. Engaging in these traditions allows pilgrims to connect more deeply with each other and the regions they pass through, making dining an essential and enriching part of the Camino experience. Whether sharing a meal with new friends in an albergue, enjoying a pilgrim menu in a local restaurant, or indulging in regional specialties, the meals enjoyed on the Camino will undoubtedly become some of the most cherished memories of the experience.

Budget-Friendly Dining Strategies

Navigating the culinary landscape of the Camino de Santiago with budget-friendly dining strategies can significantly enhance the pilgrimage experience, ensuring that meals serve as sources of nourishment, joy, and cultural immersion without breaking the bank. Leveraging meal-sharing opportunities, identifying the best-value pilgrim menus, and utilizing supermarket strategies can make dining along the Camino both affordable and memorable.

Meal-sharing serves as a cornerstone of the pilgrim experience, fostering a sense of community and camaraderie. Many albergues and local eateries encourage communal dining, where a group shares the cost of a meal. This approach reduces individual expenses and enriches the dining experience, allowing for a sampling of various dishes. Seek out establishments that offer family-style servings or "menu del día" options, which typically come at a lower price than ordering à la carte. Engaging with fellow pilgrims to plan a group meal can lead to significant savings and the opportunity to taste a broader spectrum of local cuisine, making each meal an exciting culinary experience.

Pilgrim menus, specifically designed to cater to the needs of walkers, offer substantial meals at a fixed price. These menus are common along the Camino and usually include a starter, main course, dessert, and sometimes a beverage. Maximizing the value of pilgrim menus requires discerning which establishments provide not only the best price but also the best quality and portion size. Reading reviews or asking for recommendations from locals and fellow pilgrims can guide you to places where the pilgrim menu is both satisfying and an excellent value. Some restaurants might also offer vegetarian or vegan pilgrim menus, catering to a wide range of dietary preferences without additional cost, ensuring everyone can enjoy a delightful meal.

Supermarket strategies provide a practical approach to managing meal costs while on the Camino. Purchasing ingredients to prepare your meals can be significantly cheaper than dining out. Many albergues have kitchen facilities available for pilgrims, making it possible to cook simple yet nutritious meals. Breakfast and lunch are particularly easy to manage this way, with options like local cheeses, cured meats, fresh bread, and seasonal fruits providing a cost-effective and delicious start to the day. For snacks and energy boosts along the route, consider nuts, dried fruits, and chocolate, which are calorie-dense and portable. Supermarkets also serve as great places to stock up on water and other beverages at a fraction of the cost you would pay in cafes or vending machines along the trail, allowing you to focus more on your experience. Another tip involves seeking out local markets, where fresh produce, meats, and cheeses often come at lower prices than in supermarkets. These markets not only provide opportunities to save money but also allow for engagement with local vendors and the practice of language skills, enhancing the cultural experience of the Camino. Preparing a picnic from market finds offers a delightful way to enjoy the Spanish countryside while adhering to a budget, creating cherished memories along the way.

Dining affordably on the Camino de Santiago involves a blend of social dining practices, a savvy selection of pilgrim menus, and strategic use of supermarkets and local markets. Meal-sharing with fellow pilgrims, seeking out the best-value pilgrim menus, and incorporating supermarket finds into your dining plan allow for a rich tapestry of culinary experiences without undue strain on your budget. These strategies ensure that your physical sustenance is taken care of while enriching your experience with memorable meals that reflect the spirit of the Camino—community, culture, and connection.

PART IV: ENRICHING YOUR EXPERIENCE

CHAPTER 16: THE CULTURE OF THE CAMINO

PILGRIM RITUALS & TRADITIONS

Among the most cherished rituals on the Camino de Santiago is the act of leaving a stone at Cruz de Ferro. This tradition, rich in symbolism, involves carrying a stone from one's home or the start of one's journey and placing it at the base of the iron cross located on the highest point of the Camino Francés. The stone represents a burden or a sin the pilgrim wishes to leave behind. Setting it down at Cruz de Ferro allows them to symbolically release themselves from this weight, continuing their journey with a lighter spirit. Pilgrims often take a moment of reflection here, contemplating the personal significance of the stone they have carried. This powerful act of letting go embodies the transformative potential of the Camino and reminds us that we all have the strength to move forward.

Communal meals play a central role in the pilgrim experience, fostering a sense of unity and shared purpose. These gatherings serve as moments of cultural exchange and mutual support, going beyond mere opportunities to eat. Many albergues offer communal dining options, where pilgrims can contribute ingredients or assist in meal preparation. Sitting down at a shared table allows for the exchange of stories, advice, and encouragement. Lifelong friendships often form over these meals. For many, these experiences epitomize the Camino's spirit of community, offering a profound sense of belonging and togetherness, reminding us that we are never truly alone on this path.

The practice of exchanging pilgrim greetings reinforces the camaraderie of the Camino. The traditional greeting, "Buen Camino," meaning "Good Way," is exchanged countless times each day among pilgrims. This simple phrase encapsulates a wealth of goodwill, encouragement, and shared understanding. It serves as a reminder that although the journey is personal, no one walks alone. The greeting transcends language barriers, uniting pilgrims from diverse backgrounds for a common purpose. This small but significant affirmation reflects the supportive and inclusive culture that defines the Camino, creating a space where everyone can thrive together.

These rituals and traditions enrich the Camino de Santiago with layers of meaning and connection. Engaging with them allows pilgrims to experience the journey more deeply, both as a physical trek and a spiritual quest. They provide moments of reflection, opportunities for connection, and a sense of participation in something greater than oneself. For many, these experiences rank among the most memorable and transformative aspects of the Camino, embodying the essence of the pilgrimage and its capacity to change lives for the better.

Symbolism of Shell, Staff, & Scallop Markers

The shell, often a scallop, stands out as a prominent symbol associated with the Camino de Santiago. Its historical roots trace back to the legend of Saint James, whose remains are said to be buried in Santiago de Compostela. According to lore, a knight's horse fell into the water and emerged covered in scallop shells. Since then, the scallop shell has represented the pilgrimage itself, with its grooves symbolizing the various routes pilgrims travel from across Europe, all leading to a single point: the tomb of Saint James. Today, the shell serves practical purposes as well. Pilgrims use it to scoop water from streams or as a bowl for food, embodying the simplicity and humility of the pilgrim's experience, reminding everyone that every step taken contributes to a larger story.

The staff holds significant meaning, harking back to medieval times when pilgrims carried a walking stick for support. This tool not only aided them over rugged terrain but also served as a weapon against wild animals or thieves. More importantly, the staff symbolizes the strength and resilience required to complete the pilgrimage. It serves as a reminder of the physical and spiritual support that the Camino provides, offering a sense of stability and protection. In modern times, the staff remains a common sight among pilgrims, representing their commitment and perseverance on the path and encouraging them to face each challenge with courage.

Scallop markers, painted yellow, guide the pilgrims along the Camino, ensuring they do not lose their way. These markers, often found on trees, stones, or the pavement, serve as more than directional signs; they represent the guiding hand of the Camino, leading pilgrims toward their spiritual and personal goals. The yellow scalloped marker acts as a beacon of hope and encouragement, signifying progress and direction on the path. It reassures pilgrims that they are on the right track, both literally and metaphorically, instilling a sense of confidence as they move forward.

The deep historical and spiritual significance of these symbols—the shell, staff, and scallop markers—continues to resonate with modern-day pilgrims. They are not mere relics of the past but living traditions that carry profound meanings. The shell symbolizes the purpose of the journey and the pilgrim's identity; the staff represents the support and resilience needed to face the challenges of the Camino, and the scallop markers offer guidance and reassurance. Together, these symbols form an integral part of the Camino's culture, enriching the pilgrimage experience by connecting travelers to the path's historical and spiritual dimensions.

Pilgrims who engage with these symbols can deepen their connection to the Camino. This participation links them to a centuries-old tradition, connecting them to the countless pilgrims who have walked the path before them. These symbols serve as constant reminders of the Camino's rich heritage, the communal spirit of the pilgrimage, and the personal transformation that awaits those who walk the path with an open heart. Carrying a shell, using a staff, or following the scallop markers allows pilgrims to experience the Camino not just as a physical journey but as a spiritual voyage that transcends time, uniting them with the universal quest for meaning, purpose, and connection.

Modern-Day Pilgrim Community

In the digital age, the community of modern-day pilgrims has expanded beyond the physical paths of the Camino de Santiago, creating a vibrant, interconnected network of past, present, and future pilgrims. This community thrives across various online platforms, providing a space for individuals to connect, share experiences, and seek advice, enriching the Camino experience even before it begins.

Online forums and social media groups serve as essential tools for those planning their pilgrimage. Websites dedicated to the Camino, such as the Camino de Santiago forums, offer a platform where individuals can ask questions, discuss routes, and recommend accommodations. These forums contain a wealth of information, where the collective wisdom of thousands of pilgrims is readily available. Facebook groups and WhatsApp chats facilitate real-time interaction, allowing for the exchange of tips, encouragement, and coordination of meet-ups along the route.

Blogs and personal websites provide detailed accounts of pilgrims' experiences, offering insights into the daily realities of walking the Camino. These personal narratives often include practical advice on packing, physical and mental preparation, and reflections on the spiritual and transformative aspects of the pilgrimage. Engaging with the experiences of others inspires and motivates, fostering a sense of connection to the broader pilgrim community.

Apps designed specifically for the Camino de Santiago have become invaluable resources for modern pilgrims. Route planners detail distances between stages, accommodations, and points of interest, while social apps enable pilgrims to connect with fellow travelers in real time. Apps such as Camino Pilgrim and Wise Pilgrim receive wide recommendations for their user-friendly interfaces and comprehensive information.

YouTube and podcasts provide visual and auditory means to connect with the Camino. Pilgrims share their experiences through vlogs and documentary-style videos, offering a glimpse into the daily walk and the stunning landscapes of the Camino. Podcasts feature interviews with past pilgrims, discussions on the history and culture of the Camino, and advice on preparing for the pilgrimage. These resources prove particularly useful for visualizing the experience and hearing firsthand accounts from a diverse range of perspectives.

Engaging with the modern-day pilgrim community through these digital platforms allows individuals to join a global network of support and camaraderie. This interaction creates opportunities to learn from the experiences of others, share personal insights, and form lasting connections. Whether seeking logistical advice or spiritual encouragement or simply wanting to share the excitement of the pilgrimage, the online pilgrim community serves as an accessible and invaluable resource for anyone drawn to the Camino de Santiago.

Utilizing these digital tools and platforms enables pilgrims to approach their pilgrimage with confidence, knowing they have the collective knowledge and support of a worldwide community at their fingertips. This modern approach to the ancient pilgrimage ensures that the spirit of the Camino—its traditions, camaraderie, and transformative power—continues to thrive in the 21st century, connecting hearts and minds across continents and cultures.

Respecting Local Culture & Etiquette

Respecting local culture and etiquette is paramount for pilgrims on the Camino de Santiago. This trek is not just a physical challenge but a passage through communities with deep-rooted traditions and customs. Adhering to these cultural norms ensures a harmonious experience for both pilgrims and locals. Here are essential do's and don'ts to guide your interactions and behavior along the Camino.

Do:
1. Greet Locals Warmly: A simple "Buenos días" or "Buen Camino" shows respect and friendliness toward the locals. These greetings break down barriers and often lead to meaningful exchanges, creating connections that enrich your experience.

2. Learn Basic Spanish Phrases: While many people along the Camino may speak English, attempting to communicate in Spanish is greatly appreciated. This effort demonstrates respect for the local culture and enhances your interactions, making your experience even more fulfilling.

3. Respect Sacred Sites: Many pilgrims walk the Camino for spiritual reasons, and even if you do not, showing respect at churches, shrines, and other sacred sites is important. Speak softly, dress appropriately, and behave in a manner befitting the sanctity of these places, allowing you to appreciate the deeper significance they hold for others.

4. Follow Local Dining Etiquette: Meal times in Spain typically occur later than what many are accustomed to. Lunch is often around 2-3 PM, and dinner can be as late as 9 PM. Adapting to these customs respects local practices and enriches your culinary experience on the Camino, inviting you to savor the flavors of the region.

5. Support Local Businesses: Purchasing from local markets, dining at local restaurants, and staying in family-run accommodations contribute to the communities you're passing through. This approach gives back and expresses gratitude for the hospitality, fostering a sense of community along your path.

Don't:

1. Litter: Keep the Camino clean for fellow pilgrims and locals. Always dispose of your trash properly, even if it means carrying it until you find a suitable place to throw it away. This small act of care can significantly impact the environment you're enjoying.

2. Make Excessive Noise: Many towns along the Camino are small and tranquil. Loud conversations, especially late at night or early in the morning, can be disruptive. Be mindful of your volume, particularly in accommodations shared with others, as this consideration helps maintain the peaceful atmosphere of the Camino.

3. Ignore Waymarkings: The Camino is well-marked with yellow arrows and scallop shells. Respect these markers by not defacing or ignoring them. They guide you and preserve the integrity of the trail, ensuring that everyone can enjoy this beautiful path.

4. Disrespect Private Property: While the Camino passes through many open fields and rural areas, much of the land is privately owned. Do not trespass on private property, cut through crops, or disturb livestock. Respecting these boundaries reinforces a spirit of cooperation and understanding among travelers and locals alike.

5. Forget to Queue: In Spain, queuing (lining up) is a respected practice, whether at a bakery, a supermarket, or waiting for the bathroom. Skipping the line is considered rude and disrespectful, so following this custom fosters goodwill and patience in your interactions.

Pilgrims who adhere to these do's and don'ts contribute positively to the communities they pass through. The Camino de Santiago fosters mutual respect and understanding, where interactions between pilgrims and locals can be as enriching as the experience itself. Local customs and etiquette enhance your pilgrimage and foster an environment of respect and appreciation for the diverse cultures and traditions that make the Camino de Santiago a truly unique experience. Remember that you are a guest in these regions, and your behavior should reflect gratitude and reverence for the opportunity to walk this ancient path.

CHAPTER 17: REFLECTING ON YOUR JOURNEY

CAPTURING YOUR CAMINO MEMORIES

Documenting your Camino experience serves as a personal keepsake and a way to share your transformative moments with others. Capturing memories can be a reflective practice, allowing you to process and appreciate the moments as they unfold. Here are practical ways to document your pilgrimage, ensuring that every step, landscape, and encounter is preserved in a manner that resonates with your journey.

Journaling: Keeping a daily journal is a timeless method for recording your experiences, thoughts, and feelings. Select a durable, lightweight notebook that fits easily in your backpack. Dedicate a few minutes each evening to jot down the day's events, the people you met, the challenges you faced, and the insights you gained. Note the names of places, accommodations, and any recommendations you received or can give to future pilgrims. This practice serves as a record and aids in reflection, helping you digest the day's experiences and recognize your personal growth over time.

Photography: In the age of smartphones, taking high-quality photos has never been easier. Photography captures the visual essence of your Camino experience. Take a mix of landscapes, close-up details, and portraits of fellow pilgrims and locals. Capture the essence of the Camino through its varied terrains, historical sites, and the simple yet profound moments of daily life on the trail. Remember to back up your photos regularly, using cloud storage or an external hard drive, to ensure that your memories are preserved even if your device is lost or damaged.

Creative Storytelling: Explore creative ways to document your journey beyond traditional journaling and photography. Sketching or watercolor painting captures the landscapes and moments uniquely, even if you're not a trained artist. Recording voice memos encapsulates the sounds of the Camino, from the bustling morning preparations at an albergue to the serene sounds of nature along the trail. These recordings evoke specific moments and places.

Digital Platforms: For those who want to share their journey with a wider audience, creating a blog or vlog offers a rewarding way to document your Camino. This approach combines written narratives, photos, and videos, providing a comprehensive account of your pilgrimage. Social media platforms like Instagram and Facebook work well for sharing daily snapshots and reflections, connecting you with a community of past, present, and future pilgrims.

Post-Camino Projects: After returning home, compile your writings, sketches, and photos into a personal memoir or photo book. This serves as a tangible memento of your journey and can be a meaningful gift to share with family and friends. For those who enjoy public speaking, presenting your Camino experience at local community centers, libraries, or hiking clubs can inspire others and provide a platform for reflection on the impact of your pilgrimage.

Finding the methods that resonate most with you is essential in documenting your Camino. Whether through words, images, or sounds, capturing your memories extends the Camino's impact, allowing you to revisit and share the experience long after it has ended. This practice enriches your own experience and contributes to the collective memory of the Camino, offering insights and inspiration to future generations of pilgrims.

Camino Lessons for Daily Transformation

The transformative experience of the Camino de Santiago extends far beyond the physical paths trodden by pilgrims. It encompasses a profound internal voyage that can significantly impact one's daily life and mindset long after the pilgrimage has concluded. Integrating the Camino's lessons into your everyday routine requires a conscious effort to embody the values, insights, and experiences gained along the way. This transformation can lead to a more purposeful, centered, and enriched life.

Mindfulness and Presence: One of the most powerful lessons from the Camino is the practice of mindfulness—being fully present in the moment. The simplicity of walking, the connection with nature, and the rhythm of daily life on the Camino foster a heightened state of awareness. Dedicate a few minutes each day to mindfulness or meditation. Focus on your breath, the sensations in your body, or the sounds around you. This practice can help reduce stress, enhance focus, and bring a sense of calm to your daily activities. Simplicity and Minimalism: The Camino teaches the value of simplicity and the freedom that comes from living with less. Pilgrims quickly discover the liberating feeling of carrying only what is necessary. Reflect on your material possessions and consider decluttering your living space, keeping only what serves a purpose or brings joy. This minimalist approach can lead to a clearer mind and a more focused life, emphasizing experiences over possessions.

Community and Connection: The sense of camaraderie and community on the Camino is profound. Pilgrims from all walks of life share stories, meals, and moments of support. Foster this sense of connection in your daily life by reaching out to friends, family, and community members. Volunteer, join a club or group that aligns with your interests, or simply engage more deeply with the people around you. These connections can provide invaluable support, enrich your life, and remind you that you're part of a larger community.

Resilience and Perseverance: Walking the Camino tests physical and mental endurance. It teaches resilience—the ability to face challenges head-on—and the perseverance to keep going despite difficulties. Apply these lessons to personal and professional challenges by setting goals, breaking them down into manageable steps, and celebrating progress along the way. When faced with obstacles, remember the resilience demonstrated on the Camino and approach problems with a solution-oriented mindset.

Gratitude and Appreciation: The Camino experience often leads to a profound sense of gratitude—for the beauty of nature, the kindness of strangers, and the strength of one's own body and spirit. Cultivate this sense of appreciation in your daily life by keeping a gratitude journal. Each day, write down three things you're grateful for. This practice can shift your focus from what's lacking to the abundance present in your life, fostering a positive outlook and greater happiness.

Reflection and Personal Growth: The Camino provides ample time for reflection, allowing pilgrims to contemplate life's big questions and their values. Set aside time each week to contemplate your goals, values, and the direction of your life. Consider how your actions align with your values and how you can live more authentically. This ongoing self-reflection can guide personal growth and ensure that your life path reflects your true self.

Incorporating the Camino's lessons into your daily routine and mindset requires intention, effort, and commitment. Embodying the principles learned along the Camino enables you to navigate life with greater purpose, fulfillment, and connection. The Camino illustrates that every step, no matter how small, contributes to personal transformation, allowing you to carry the spirit of the Camino with you every day.

Staying Connected & Future Pilgrimages

Staying connected with the Camino community and planning future pilgrimages play essential roles in extending the transformative experience of the Camino de Santiago. The experience does not conclude at Santiago de Compostela; it marks the beginning of a new chapter where the lessons learned and connections made continue to enrich one's life. Engaging with the Camino community can take various forms, such as participating in online forums or attending pilgrim reunions, each offering unique opportunities to share stories and insights and plan subsequent experiences.

Online forums and social media groups dedicated to the Camino de Santiago serve as valuable resources for information and camaraderie. Platforms like the Camino de Santiago forums or Facebook groups create spaces for pilgrims to ask questions, share experiences, and offer advice. These digital communities welcome both novices seeking guidance for their first pilgrimage and seasoned veterans sharing wisdom from multiple journeys. Involvement in these communities fosters a continuous connection to the Camino spirit, helping to maintain a sense of adventure and discovery in daily life.

Pilgrim reunions provide another way to nurture and celebrate the bonds formed on the Camino. These gatherings, often organized by Camino societies or informal groups, unite individuals who share the common bond of having walked the Camino. They offer opportunities to reminisce about past journeys, exchange stories, and inspire each other for future pilgrimages. Attending these reunions can reignite the pilgrim spirit, offering motivation and companionship for planning the next Camino experience.

Planning future pilgrimages naturally follows for many who have walked the Camino de Santiago. The desire to return can be strong, whether to experience a different route, revisit favorite places, or seek new challenges. When considering a subsequent pilgrimage, reflect on which aspects of the Camino were most meaningful. Was it the physical challenge, the spiritual introspection, the cultural immersion, or the connections with fellow pilgrims? Identifying these elements can guide the planning of your next experience, ensuring it aligns with your personal growth and aspirations.

Exploring different routes allows for the chance to see new landscapes, discover hidden gems, and understand the broader historical and cultural pilgrimage context. Each route possesses its unique character and set of challenges, from the popular Camino Francés to the solitary Via de la Plata or the rugged beauty of the Camino del Norte. Researching these routes, grasping their historical significance, and preparing for their specific demands can transform the planning process into an enriching experience. Reflecting on the lessons learned from previous pilgrimages proves crucial in planning future walks. Consider what worked well and what could be improved, whether adjusting your packing list, choosing different accommodations, or allowing more time for reflection and exploration. Engaging with the Camino community provides valuable insights and recommendations to enhance your next pilgrimage.

Think about how you can contribute to the Camino community. Sharing your experiences through blog posts, social media, speaking at pilgrim gatherings, or volunteering with Camino organizations can guide and inspire future pilgrims. Your journey on the Camino de Santiago tells a story of personal transformation and connection, offering hope, encouragement, and practical advice to others on their pilgrimage.

Connecting with the Camino community and planning future pilgrimages keeps the spirit of the Camino alive in your heart and daily life. Through online forums, pilgrim reunions, and thoughtful preparation for new experiences, you can continue to grow, learn, and share the profound impact of this timeless path. The Camino invites pilgrims to explore, reflect, and connect in ways that enrich their understanding of the world and themselves.

Made in United States
North Haven, CT
19 June 2025

69942345R00057